lonely planet

POCKET MIAMI

Jesse Scott

Contents

Top: Lifeguard tower, South Beach (p44)
Bottom: Hotels, Ocean Drive (p43)

Plan Your Trip 4

Explore Miami 33

Miami Toolkit 143

★ Top Experiences

FROM TOP LEFT: IGOR LINK/SHUTTERSTOCK, MARIAKRAY/SHUTTERSTOCK

The Journey Begins Here

Growing up in Fredericksburg, Virginia, South Florida was my family's annual Christmas destination. My parents drove 14.5 hours straight to my grandpa's house in Fort Lauderdale, a place I cherished – the warmth of family, sunny weather and endless adventures. My grandpa's influence and fond memories surely played a part in leading my wife and me to call South Florida home now for nearly a decade. As a local journalist, I've explored Miami and well beyond for several top outlets. My discoveries form an ongoing love letter to this vibrant, diverse and culinary-rich region – a letter that is still being written.

Jesse Scott
@jesserobertscott

Jesse is a South Florida-based writer who has written about food, entertainment, culture, travel and their intersections for 20-plus years.

LAZYLLAMA/SHUTTERSTOCK

THE BEST

Beach Experiences

Miami's beaches are always inviting—cooler in winter, sizzling in summer, and always there. They're the city's tranquil heartbeat, with architectural marvels embracing the view and even the most indoorsy visitors eventually drawn to the water's edge.

People-watch around the clock at Miami's **South Beach**, with sunrises and painted lifeguard stations filling out the landscape. (p44)

Sunbathe with your clothes on – or not – and watch boats big and small coast by at **Haulover Beach Park** (pictured), tucked on the northern end of Miami Beach. (p44)

Dabble in nature trails or stay put on the sand at **Crandon Park** (pictured) on Key Biscayne, a blissfully quiet and quick retreat from Miami's endless energy. (p140)

Truly chill – perhaps with little ones in tow – along **North Beach**, a stretch of quaint family-friendly beaches. (p44)

Spot a manatee as you plop on a peaceful stretch of **Virginia Key Beach North Point Park** – perhaps you'll see some colorful birds squawking, too. (p140)

Right: Lifeguard tower, South Beach (p44)

THE BEST

Water Experiences

Miami's waters always call – kayak through mangroves, snorkel vibrant reefs or speed across Biscayne Bay. Paddleboarders, anglers and divers explore endless worlds, from sunken shipwrecks to trophy fishing. The tides promise something for everyone.

Float around for the day at **Venetian Pool** in Coral Gables, a quarry-gone-poolscape with caves, rock formations and more. (p122)

Watch eagles fly by during a boat trip to **Oleta River State Park's** mangrove island (pictured). (p46)

Kayak or canoe through mangroves in **Everglades National Park** (p134), keeping an eye out for wildlife like ospreys, bald eagles, loggerhead turtles and great blue herons.

Hop on a guided pontoon boat tour from **Dinner Key Marina** in Coconut Grove to offshore destinations like Stiltsville and Boca Chita Key. (p111)

Stroll the **Miami Riverwalk** (pictured), watching tiny and mega watercrafts float by, with the Brickell and Downtown skylines as a backdrop. (p67)

Right: Dinner Key (p111)

FROM LEFT: FOTOLUMINATE LLC/SHUTTERSTOCK, FOTOLUMINATE LLC/SHUTTERSTOCK, FRANCISCO BLANCO/SHUTTERSTOCK

THE BEST

Island Experiences

Miami's islands add another layer to the swaying palm landscape, dotting the coast like a gem-studded necklace. Often with natural beauty and laid-back charm, they offer a perfect escape just off the mainland.

Venture off Coconut Grove's southern shore to the island portion off **Dinner Key Marina**, with canopied nooks that are primed for a picnic. (p111)

Hop by bridge from Miami to **Key Biscayne** for covered trails, a nature center tour and a selfie session at an iconic lighthouse. (p140)

Take a tour and gawk at some of Miami's millionaire and billionaire havens, including **Fisher Island**, **Star Island** and **Millionaire's Row**. (p65)

Listen to the chorus of capybaras, lemurs, sloths and more on **Jungle Island** – embark on a treetop trek above it all, too. (p65)

Peruse the tiny yet skyscraper-draped island that is **Brickell Key**, just a stone's throw from Miami's burgeoning Brickell financial district. (p66)

Lighthouse, Key Biscayne (p140)

LUCKY-PHOTOGRAPHER/SHUTTERSTOCK

THE BEST

Cultural Experiences

Miami's cultural fabric is vibrant, shaped by indigenous roots and a melting pot of Latin American influences. Even its unique Spanglish reflects the city's distinct ethos – where everyone, lovingly, is a 'bro.'

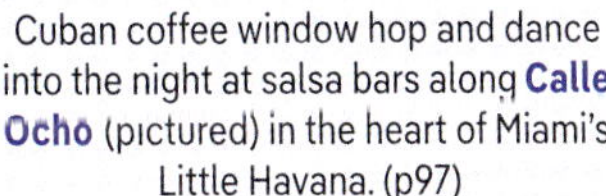

Cuban coffee window hop and dance into the night at salsa bars along **Calle Ocho** (pictured) in the heart of Miami's Little Havana. (p97)

Browse Haitian sculptures and art and, perhaps, take a folk dancing class at the **Little Haiti Cultural Center**. (p132)

Pop over to the Allapattah neighborhood and spend hours perusing adjoining museums **Superblue Miami** and **Rubell Museum**. (p90)

Visit the grounds of one of South Florida's most famous tribes and watch an alligator-wrestling demonstration (pictured) at **Miccosukee Indian Village**. (p137)

Museum-hop around town, from the traditional to the wilder and trendier, eg the **World Erotic Art Museum** and **Museum of Ice Cream**. (p47)

FROM LEFT: FOTOLUMINATE LLC/SHUTTERSTOCK, SERGEY AKHRAMEEV/SHUTTERSTOCK

THE BEST

Art Experiences

Miami's art scene is as bold as its geography – Wynwood's walls burst with color, Cuban masters shine in Little Havana and creativity spills onto every sun-soaked surface.

Marvel at contemporary art, thought-provoking exhibits and Biscayne Bay views at **Pérez Art Museum Miami**. (p56)

Step into Miami's most vibrant outdoor gallery at **Wynwood Walls**, where world-famous street artists turn warehouse walls into works of urban art (pictured). (p76)

Wander through a repurposed warehouse packed with a family-owned collection of bold contemporary art at the **Rubell Museum**. (p88)

Before seeing art deco masterpieces in South Beach and beyond, pop into the **Art Deco Museum & Welcome Center** (pictured) to learn about the craft firsthand. (p43)

Peruse the region's up-and-coming talent, or take an art class yourself, at **Oolite Arts** in Miami Beach. (p48)

Right: *Chaos SAS* by Jedd Novatt, Pérez Art Museum Miami (p56)

FROM LEFT: DEIDRE DESIGN/SHUTTERSTOCK, ZIMMYTWS/SHUTTERSTOCK, 365 FOCUS PHOTOGRAPHY/SHUTTERSTOCK

THE BEST

Seafood Experiences

From dockside dives to upscale oceanfront feasts, seafood is a menu staple everywhere here. Stone crab, conch fritters and seared mahi tell stories of coastal bounty, served with soul, sunshine and perhaps a squeeze of lime.

Gawk at a flaming lobster thermidor – which is literally ignited on your table – at the sultry and hip **Giselle**. (p70)

Crack into world-famous claws at **Joe's Stone Crab** (pictured) – a Miami institution since 1913 – and save room for the key lime pie. (p49)

Indulge in the freshest catches at **La Camaronera Seafood Joint and Fish Market** (pictured) in Little Havana, spanning Gulf Coast shrimp to local snapper. (p101)

Nosh on just-shucked oysters or other seafood delights just off the Miami River at **River Oyster Bar**. (p70)

Right: Oysters

FROM LEFT: AMPARO FONTANET/SHUTTERSTOCK, JEFFREY ISAAC GREENBERG 13+/ALAMY STOCK PHOTO, JANCZAKO/SHUTTERSTOCK

New World Symphony (p47)

THE BEST

Live Music Experiences

Island grooves, Latin beats and mega-DJs fuel Miami's vibrant nights. Salsa spills onto Calle Ocho, punk and funk electrify Wynwood and tiki-lit beach bars at hotels sway to the jams. This is a city where every night pulses with a unique rhythm.

Watch Broadway hits and orchestral spectacles at the **Adrienne Arsht Center for the Performing Arts**, Miami's premier performing arts hub. (p58)

Sip on mojitos, listen to live jazz, get moving to some salsa and perhaps dance on the bar at **Ball & Chain** in Little Havana. (p98)

Experience classical music reimagined, with an open-air Wallcast concert – projecting live performances onto an outdoor screen – at a **New World Symphony** show. (p47)

Spend an evening with the **Miami City Ballet** – one of the most renowned in the US – at the Ophelia & Juan Js. Roca Center. (p48)

Immerse yourself in 'Old Cuba' at **Café La Trova** along Calle Ocho and enjoy some of the most celebrated cocktails in town while you're at it. (p98)

Best for Kids

Spend the day splashing about in Miami's loveliest swimming pool, the **Venetian Pool** (p122) in Coral Gables, which resembles a Roman emperor's playground.

Set up at a picnic table in front of a pretty sweep of beach at **Bill Baggs Cape Florida State Park**, plus enjoy scenic walks among the greenery.

Visit **Miami Children's Museum** (p67), an indoor playland where kids can go on many imaginary adventures (including under the sea).

Spend a day at **Phillip & Patricia Frost Museum of Science** (p67), which has an aquarium, a planetarium and hands-on exhibits exploring the world's natural wonders.

Peruse aquarium exhibits, embark on short nature trails and sign up for monthly kid-focused outdoor activities at **Marjory Stoneman Douglas Biscayne Nature Center** (p141).

Best for Free

Catch free outdoor film screenings and concert simulcasts at **SoundScape Park** (p48) throughout the year in South Beach, where the open-air setting makes for a perfect night under the stars.

Stroll around the bustling kiosks at **Wynwood Marketplace** (p80), listen to live performances and soak up the neighborhood's vibrant street art and creative energy.

Head to **South Pointe Park** (p48), the southernmost tip of Miami Beach, for a family-friendly seaside escape, complete with walking paths, scenic views and a breezy pier.

Saunter along the **Miami Beach Boardwalk** (p44) and enjoy an ever-changing mix of ocean views, quirky people and lively beachfront activity all year long.

Explore the grand public spaces of the **Biltmore Hotel** (p126) in Coral Gables at your leisure or join a free Sunday tour at 2pm filled with fascinating history and fun facts.

Three Perfect Days

Explore Miami's glitz, vibrant beaches, cultural hubs and trendy enclaves in this all-in-one itinerary, blending luxury, diversity and hipster hot spots for the ultimate city experience.

Carlyle hotel (p43), Ocean Drive

DAY ONE

Only Have One Day?

MORNING

What is a Miami trip without the beach? Start in **South Beach** (pictured; p44) and use this art deco hub and its mix of classic and amenity-filled hotels as your base. Begin with an overview of all things deco by taking a walking tour with the **Art Deco Museum & Welcome Center** (p43).

AFTERNOON

Visit the **Wolfsonian-FIU** (p43) for its excellent exhibitions on decorative arts, industrial design and architecture. Build in some time for lounging on the beach.

EVENING

Dress for a comfortable stroll and head to **Lincoln Rd** (p46) to people-watch and browse the trendy shops and restaurants. Nightcap with a memorable cocktail at **Sweet Liberty** (p50)

FROM LEFT: SERGIO TB/SHUTTERSTOCK, MIA2YOU/SHUTTERSTOCK, BLUEEE77/SHUTTERSTOCK, FOTOLUMINATE LLC/SHUTTERSTOCK

DAY TWO

A Weekend Trip

MORNING

The next day visit the galleries and shops of **Wynwood** and the **Design District** (p73). Start off with a visit to **Wynwood Walls** (p76), an ever-changing art installation of vibrant wall-sized murals.

AFTERNOON

Stop for an early-afternoon espresso at **Panther Coffee** (pictured; p86) and tacos at **Coyo Taco**, then continue your saunter through hip Wynwood, gawking at graffiti-clad buildings.

EVENING

Head to the Design District to peruse public art installations that glisten amid the sunset, while popping into high-end galleries – buy if the budget is there. At night, grab a bite and drinks at **1-800 Lucky** (p85) back In Wynwood.

DAY THREE

A Short Break

MORNING

Head to **Little Havana** (p93) for a *cafecito* (small shot of Cuban coffee) at the *ventanita* (ordering window) of your choice; **Versailles** (p100) is a generational favorite. Along Calle Ocho, pop into **Máximo Gómez Park** (p100) to watch locals play dominos (pictured).

AFTERNOON

Bump down to **Coral Gables** (p117) and visit the Mediterranean-Inspired mansions, prioritizing a stop by **Vizcaya Museum & Gardens** (p105), a massive bayfront estate. Take a sunset cruise on Biscayne Bay if time allows.

EVENING

Get in on Miami's nightlife. Stroll along **Ocean Drive** (p43) to take in neon-draped buildings and, should your heart desire, a lounge-y evening at the multifaceted **MILA** (p49). Keep the party going at **Sweet Liberty** (p50), one of Miami Beach's coolest cocktail havens.

If You Have More Time

Explore Coconut Grove's **Kampong** (p110), a lush tropical garden filled with exotic plants, once home to famed horticulturist David Fairchild. From there, neighboring Coral Gables is loaded with exquisite, Mediterranean-inspired architecture. You'll want to take a dip (or better part of an afternoon) sitting poolside at the rock landscape-draped and expansive **Venetian Pool** (p122).

Venture to Allapattah's **Rubell Museum** (p88), showcasing contemporary masterpieces, or, across the street, explore the immersive **Superblue Miami** (p90) experience, where art and technology blend.

For a laid-back beach alternative, visit **North Beach** (p44), a quieter stretch of sand with a charming small-town feel. Continue south to Mid-Beach and stroll along the scenic **boardwalk** (p44) overlooking the waves, passing by iconic beachfront hotels. If you're seeking history, visit the **Biltmore Hotel** (p126) in Coral Gables, an architectural gem with a storied past and legendary tales of glamour.

Make sure to catch a Broadway-esque show at the **Adrienne Arsht Center for the Performing Arts** (p58) or, for some Latin flair, hit **Ball & Chain** (p98) or **Café La Trova** (p98) along Calle Ocho for live music and never-ending energy.

Kampong (p110)

A Day Trip

By car, venture deep into the Everglades along the legendary Tamiami Trail (US 41). From Miami, head west, making a pit stop for an airboat ride and a snack at a quirky roadside restaurant. From there, visit **Shark Valley** (p136), perhaps the most popular entrance to **Everglades National Park** (p134). Hop on a **Shark Valley tram tour** (p136) for a guided ride through sawgrass marshes or rent a bicycle and follow the 15-mile loop, sharing the road with alligators sunning. Departing the park and before heading back to Miami, detour to the **Miccosukee Indian Village** (p137), which has a museum showcasing historical and current like. On-site, check out an ethical alligator demonstration, showcasing the importance of the creature to the tribe.

On a Rainy Day

Miami has no shortage of ways to stay entertained when the skies turn gray. The **Pérez Art Museum Miami** (p56) (locally known as PAMM) has ever-changing, contemporary exhibitions with stellar views of Biscayne Bay, while the **Wolfsonian-FIU** (pictured; p43) in South Beach showcases thought-provoking collections on design and propaganda. History buffs can explore **HistoryMiami** (p68), which brings the city's diverse past to life through exhibits on everything from aviation to immigration. For science lovers, the **Phillip & Patricia Frost Museum of Science** (p67) features a planetarium and an open-air aquarium. If museums aren't your thing, you can always ride the free **Metromover** for a scenic, rainproof city tour.

Get Prepared

BOOK AHEAD

Three months before
Reserve tickets for big-name concerts, major sporting events and top dining spots like Joe's Stone Crab or Komodo, if possible.

One month before
Book tables at popular restaurants, secure sunset cruise tickets on Biscayne Bay and grab spots for experiences like Superblue Miami.

One week before
This should be enough time to book museum entry, art deco walking tours and last-minute reservations at trendy cocktail bars.

Manners Matter

Most Floridians are quite cordial and will happily share insights into their local attractions, restaurants and drinking spots. Locals tend to avoid topics like politics and instead talk sports. With local pro teams, college powerhouses and loyalties to Caribbean teams, there's always something afoot. In the suburbs and less-busy areas (such as state parksor Everglades National Park trails), it's common to say hello to people you see.

Senior Discounts

Florida – and certainly including Miami – is a retirement haven for senior citizens. With being a senior can come some discounts across hotels, experiences and dining. Many retailers offer perks, often in the five to 30-plus percent range, to those who've earned the privilege. Minimum qualifying ages range from 50 to 65. If signage isn't visible, ask a retailer if you qualify.

Things to Know

Sales Tax Florida's sales tax sits at 6%, with additional local taxes often bringing it slightly higher. Expect to pay tax on most goods, services, restaurant meals and attraction tickets, so factor this into your budget.

ATMs Widely available across Miami; fees can add up quickly. Local banks often charge $3 to $5 per withdrawal, plus any fees from your own bank. Using credit cards where possible can help reduce cash withdrawal costs.

Currency Exchange Credit card transactions typically offer better exchange rates than airport kiosks or hotels. ATMs also provide competitive rates. For large sums, consider professional exchange services for better rates.

Save on a Water Adventure Skip expensive private boat tours by opting for public ferries or group charters. The Island Queen Cruise, for example, offers scenic views at a fraction of luxury tour prices.

TIPPING

Miami is a hospitality and service-centric city – tips are broadly encouraged across most facets of daily and tourist life, unless signage indicates a tip has already been included in a price.

Restaurants & cocktail bars
for good service

Other bars & cafes
per drink

Taxis & rideshares
for good service

Valet staff
per time

DAILY BUDGET

BUDGET: Less than $200

- Hostel dorm bed: **$60–80**
- Casual Cuban meal in Little Havana: **$10–20**
- Museum admission: **$10–20**
- Public transport day pass: **$5–6**

MIDRANGE: $200–500

- Standard hotel room: **$150–300**
- Two-course meal with drinks at a midrange restaurant: **$70–100**
- Ticket to a Miami Heat game: **from $50**
- Group Biscayne Bay cruise: **from $30**

TOP END: More than $500

- Luxury hotel or oceanfront resort: **from $400**
- Fine dining experience: **per person from $150**
- VIP nightclub table: **minimum spend $1000**
- Private yacht rental for half-day: **$800-plus**

Currency
USD ($)

Language
English and widespread Spanish

Time Zone
Eastern Standard Time (GMT/UTC plus 10 hours)

SUROROV_ALEX/SHUTTERSTOCK

TIP

The **Go City Miami Pass** *(gocity.com)* has big savings on top attractions, including Everglades tours and boat cruises. You can choose an all-inclusive or explorer-esque pass to bundle experiences and save compared to individual ticket prices.

When To Go

Anytime. Snowbirds flock for pleasant temps in the winter, the summer scorches out the crowds and cultural spectacles enthrall year-round.

Miami sizzles around the clock but timing your visit can shape your experience. Winter draws snowbirds and festivalgoers, with Art Deco Weekend bringing the city's iconic architecture to life. Locals favor late spring (April to early June) for warm waters and thinner crowds. By late summer hurricane season looms, but those who visit enjoy quieter beaches and a different kind of tropical charm. Autumn is a hidden gem – October marks the return of stone crab season, and the city hums with a relaxed, postsummer energy perfect for exploring without the high-season bustle.

The Big Events

February The **South Beach Wine & Food Festival** (SOBEWFF) is a nearly week-long, star-studded feast with celebrity chefs, beachfront tastings, cooking demos and exclusive dining experiences.

March Miami pulses with electronic beats during **Miami Music Week**, when resort pools, intimate venues and mega arenas host world-class DJs. The week culminates in the **Ultra Music Festival**, an electrifying three-day event.

May The streets of Miami Gardens transform into a high-speed spectacle for the **Miami Grand Prix**. Formula 1 cars race through the Hard Rock Stadium complex, while an entire week of celebrity-packed parties ignites the city.

December **Art Basel Miami Beach** is the crown jewel of **Miami Art Week**, bringing international artists, collectors and VIPs to the city. Beyond the galleries expect nonstop parties, immersive installations and art-inspired dinners.

Miami Weather

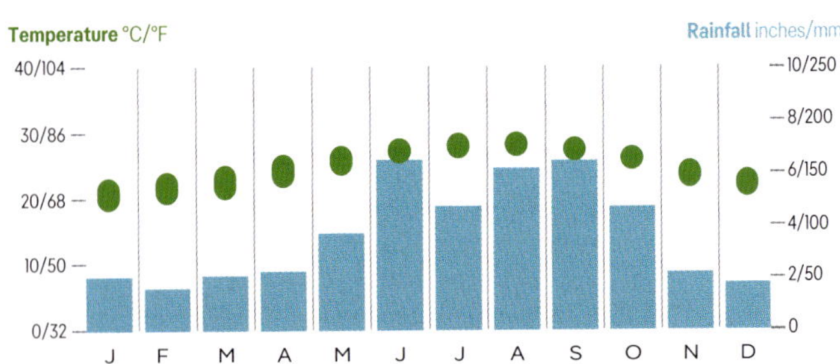

Art Deco Weekend

Local & Quirky

January Step back in time on Ocean Dr during **Art Deco Weekend**, a lively tribute to Miami Beach's 1920s and '30s architecture. Classic cars, vintage fashion and historic walking tours celebrate the city's iconic pastel-hued charm.

February One of Miami's most beloved traditions, the **Coconut Grove Arts Festival**, transforms the waterfront into an open-air gallery. Local and international artists showcase paintings, sculptures and photography, while live music and culinary experiences add to the creative buzz.

March The **Calle Ocho Music Festival**, the largest Latin music festival in the US, fills Little Havana with performances, dancing in the street and vibrant cultural spectacles. It's the ultimate fiesta.

November Literary lovers unite for the **Miami Book Fair**, a week-plus-long celebration of storytelling featuring global authors, panel discussions and a super-sized street fair with booksellers, poetry readings and special events.

ACCOMMODATIONS LOWDOWN

Expect peak rates during winter, especially around Miami Art Week and other festivals. Summer sees lower prices, but deals are best in late spring and early fall. Hurricane season (June through November) can bring stellar deals, but keep an eye on the weather.

Getting There

Most travelers reach Miami via Miami International Airport (MIA), a major international hub that connects the broader region. Fort Lauderdale-Hollywood International Airport (FLL) also serves the area.

From Miami International Airport to the City Center

By Bus

Miami-Dade Transit's Route 150 Airport Express bus departs every 20 to 30 minutes from MIA. It runs daily between 6am and 11:40pm The journey takes 40 minutes, depending on traffic, and costs $2.25. Buses leave from Miami Central Station, accessible via the free MIA Mover from the airport terminals. You can pay with exact cash or a loaded EASY Card, available at vending machines inside the station.

By MIA Mover

For a fast, seamless ride, take the Orange Line Metrorail from MIA. Board the free MIA Mover to Miami Central Station, where trains depart every 10 to 15 minutes. Ride the Orange Line toward Downtown, disembarking at Government Center Station after a 15-minute trip. From there, transfer to the free Metromover, a fully automated train looping around Downtown Miami. This option is ideal for travelers headed to Downtown and Brickell. The total fare is $2.25.

By Taxi or Rideshare

Taxis charge a flat rate of $30 to $35 to Downtown, taking 20 minutes in light traffic. Rideshare services have designated pickup zones outside the arrivals level. Expect fares between $20 to $40.

Other Points of Entry

Fort Lauderdale-Hollywood International Airport

Rideshare services and taxis provide the quickest route to Miami's city center from FLL, taking around 40 minutes and costing $50 to $80. For a budget option, there is a shuttle from FLL to the nearby Tri-Rail Fort Lauderdale Airport station, with trains running every 30 to 60 minutes. The journey takes about an hour to Miami's confines and costs $5.

Brightline Train

From points north, including Orlando, West Palm Beach and Fort Lauderdale, Brightline offers a high-speed ride to Miami's city center. Trains run every 30 to 60 minutes. Fares can start at $10 each way and may be more expensive based on demand.

Getting Around

Getting around Miami is easiest by car, though traffic can be heavy during rush hour. Public transit, including Metrorail, Metromover and buses, offers budget-friendly options for key areas. Rideshares and taxis provide flexibility, while bike rentals and scooters are ideal for short trips. Walking is also a great option in pedestrian-friendly areas like Wynwood and South Beach.

Taxis & Rideshares

Taxis are available in Miami, but they can be expensive and hard to hail on the street. Most people rely on rideshare services like Uber and Lyft, which offer more competitive pricing and convenient app-based bookings. A 20-minute ride within the city can cost from $20 to $40, depending on traffic and demand. While taxis have fixed rates from the airport, rideshares typically provide cheaper alternatives.

Metrorail & Metromover

Miami's Metrorail is a fast and affordable option for getting around key areas, including Downtown, Brickell and the airport. The Orange and Green lines run daily, with fares at $2.25 per ride. At Government Center Station, passengers can transfer to the Metromover, a free

automated train that loops through Downtown and Brickell, making it easy to explore the city without spending a dime.

Metrobus

Miami-Dade's Metrobus system covers a large area, including Miami Beach and surrounding suburbs. Fares start at $2.25, and payment can be made via cash or an EASY

FROM LEFT: JUST DANCE/SHUTTERSTOCK, BILANOL/SHUTTERSTOCK

ESSENTIAL APP

Download the **GO Miami-Dade Transit App** to plan travel across the city's Metrorail, Metrobus and Metromover systems.

Card. Buses run frequently but can be slow due to traffic. While useful for budget travelers, longer trips often take more time than expected.

Trolley

Miami's free trolley system is a convenient way to travel through neighborhoods like Coral Gables, Little Havana and Downtown. The service runs daily, with trolleys arriving every 10 to 15 minutes. Miami Beach also operates its own trolley, making it an easy way to navigate that area without needing a car.

Bicycles & E-Scooters

Miami's Citi Bike program allows visitors to rent bikes for short trips, but the city's car-heavy streets and limited bike lanes can make navigating a challenge. E-scooters, available in select areas, are an efficient way to explore short distances, especially along South Beach and Downtown.

Walking

Areas like South Beach, Wynwood and Brickell are pedestrian friendly. Sidewalks can be inconsistent outside of tourist hubs, but if you're staying in a central location, walking is a great way to experience the city's streets.

Driving & Parking

While having a car provides flexibility, Miami's traffic – especially during rush hour – can be horrible. Parking in busy areas like South Beach and Downtown is expensive and limited. Hotels often charge high valet fees, making alternative transport options more appealing for visitors staying in central areas.

Public Transport Essentials

Fares & Tickets

Miami-Dade Transit operates Metrorail, Metromover and Metrobus under a unified ticketing system. Passengers can pay fares using an EASY Card, EASY Ticket, contactless credit/debit card or mobile wallet like Apple Pay and Google Pay. A single ride on Metrorail or Metrobus costs $2.25 with unlimited ride passes also available. The EASY Card is a reusable smart card that costs $2 and can be loaded with stored value or passes. An EASY Ticket is a disposable paper card valid for up to 60 days. For visitors, a Day Pass costs $5.65 and grants unlimited travel for 24 hours, while a 7-Day Pass ($29.25) grants unlimited rides for a full week. Seniors, students and riders with accessibility needs may qualify for discounted fares with proper identification.

Where to Buy & How to Use

EASY Cards and EASY Tickets can be purchased at vending machines in Metrorail stations, online and at some supermarkets and convenience stores. To use them, you tap the card or ticket at Metrorail fare gates or on bus fareboxes. Contactless credit and debit cards function in the same way. Metrorail stations also have vending machines for balance increases.

Transfers & Savings

Passengers using an EASY Card or Ticket get free transfers between Metrobus and Metrorail within a three-hour window. Riders paying with contactless credit or debit cards also benefit without needing to carry cash or purchase tickets in advance. These options make public transport more efficient, particularly for travelers staying in central areas or those needed to make multiple transfers.

AVOID CASH ON METROBUS

Avoid using cash on Metrobus. Drivers don't provide change and the exact fare is required for boarding.

TICKETS

Miami-Dade Transit uses an integrated fare system for Metrorail and Metrobus. Passengers can pay with an EASY Card, EASY Ticket or contactless payment.

Single ride	$2.25
1-day pass	$5.65
7-day pass	$29.25
1-month pass	$112.50
Discounted fare (Seniors, Students, Accessibility Needs)	$1.10

TICKET ZONES

Miami's public transit system primarily serves three key areas. Downtown & Brickell form the central hub, with free Metromover service and multiple transit connections. Greater Miami, including Miami Beach, Coral Gables and Little Havana, is covered by Metrobus and Metrorail. Outer Miami-Dade, including suburban areas and Miami International Airport, has Metrobus and limited Metrorail access. Fares are the same across all areas.

A Few Surprises

Miami is a true cultural melting pot, with unique artists, critters, architecture and residents looming at seemingly every corner.

The Bridges That Connect It All

Causeways – roadways built over the water – define Miami's geography, linking the mainland to barrier islands and waterfront neighborhoods. They are each cultural and engineering marvels in their own right throughout Magic City.

The **MacArthur Causeway** connects Downtown to Miami Beach, offering spectacular skyline views with yachts drifting near **Star Island** (p65). The **Julia Tuttle Causeway** (Interstate 195) provides a direct route from Midtown to Miami Beach, cutting across Biscayne Bay. The **Venetian Causeway**, a scenic stretch of bridges and small islands, is ideal for cyclists and joggers. Meanwhile, the **Rickenbacker Causeway** leads to Key Biscayne, where beaches, parks and waterfront bike paths offer a quick escape from city life.

The Orange Faces of Atomik

As you explore Miami, keep an eye out for a mischievous, wide-grinning orange face staring back at you. This is the work of **Atomik**, a prolific local street artist whose signature citrus character pops up on buildings, dumpsters, road signs and even freight trains. Inspired by Florida's old Orange Bird mascot, Atomik's work is a staple of Miami's urban landscape. His most recognizable murals can be found donning Wynwood's warehouse-esque facades, but his artwork is scattered all over the city – sometimes in places you'd least expect – making every sighting feel like a new discovery.

OFFBEAT MIAMI

Ride an airboat through the **Everglades** (p134), skimming across the marshes while spotting alligators and rare birds in the wild.

Step inside the **Ancient Spanish Monastery**, a 12th-century European cloister shipped from Spain and rebuilt in North Miami Beach.

Visit the **Coral Castle**, a bizarre hand-carved limestone sculpture garden built single-handedly by a mysterious man in the 1920s.

Swim in the **Venetian Pool** (p122), a historic spring-fed oasis carved from a coral rock quarry in Coral Gables.

Roosters on Calle Ocho

The Roosters of Little Havana

Brightly painted rooster statues line Calle Ocho in Little Havana, celebrating Cuban culture, where roosters symbolize strength and pride. Originally placed by local businesses, these fiberglass birds have become neighborhood icons, with the most famous one standing outside **El Pub Restaurant** (1548 SW 8th St). But not all of Miami's roosters are sculptures – real-life roosters roam freely in Little Havana and Coconut Grove, descendants of birds once kept for cockfighting or backyard farming. Today, they strut through alleyways and residential streets, adding to Miami's forever vibrant and generally unpredictable pizzazz.

Stiltsville: Miami's Floating Relics

A mile offshore in Biscayne Bay, a handful of wooden houses stand on stilts, remnants of a once-thriving, off-the-grid community. Known as **Stiltsville** (p68), these structures date back to the 1930s, when they served as hideaways for gamblers and partygoers. Over the years, hurricanes have destroyed most of them, leaving only seven standing. While you can't visit Stiltsville without a boat, guided tours through the **Biscayne National Park Institute** (p110) provide an up-close look at this eerie, weathered slice of Miami history.

Explore Miami

Worth a Trip

Miami's Walking Tours

FRANK_PETERS/SHUTTERSTOCK

See p49
for eating, drinking and shopping listings

Explore Miami Beach

When people think of 'Miami,' they're often picturing Miami Beach – a city of stunning shorelines, art deco charm, high-end boutiques and buzzing nightlife. Beyond the glitz, Miami Beach offers laid-back bars, great dining and cultural gems, all set against pastel-hued deco buildings and swaying palms. Here, you can craft your perfect experience: jog at sunrise; do yoga and catch a concert; or sleep in, shop, dine by the water and dance until dawn. From the energy of South Beach to the relaxed vibes of North Beach, Miami Beach delivers an iconic blend of luxury and leisure.

Getting Around

Metrobus Route 120 (Beach MAX) operates daily, connecting Aventura Mall to the northeast to Downtown via Miami Beach, including South Beach. This convenient route is favored by both visitors and residents.

The Venetian Causeway is a cyclist-friendly route linking Miami Beach to the mainland. It features dedicated bike lanes and low speed limits, providing a scenic and safe journey across Biscayne Bay.

Water Taxi Miami offers ferry services between South Beach and the Bayside Marketplace in Downtown Miami, providing a scenic and reliable alternative to traversing a causeway by car.

THE BEST

PEOPLE-WATCHING South Beach (p44)

QUINTESSENTIALLY MIAMI BEACH MUSEUM Art Deco Museum and Welcome Center (p43)

PLACE FOR A STROLL Miami Beach Boardwalk (p44)

NATURE-INFUSED PARK Oleta River State Park (p46)

BEACH FOR EVERYONE Haulover Beach Park (p44)

South Beach (p44)

LAZYLLAMA/SHUTTERSTOCK

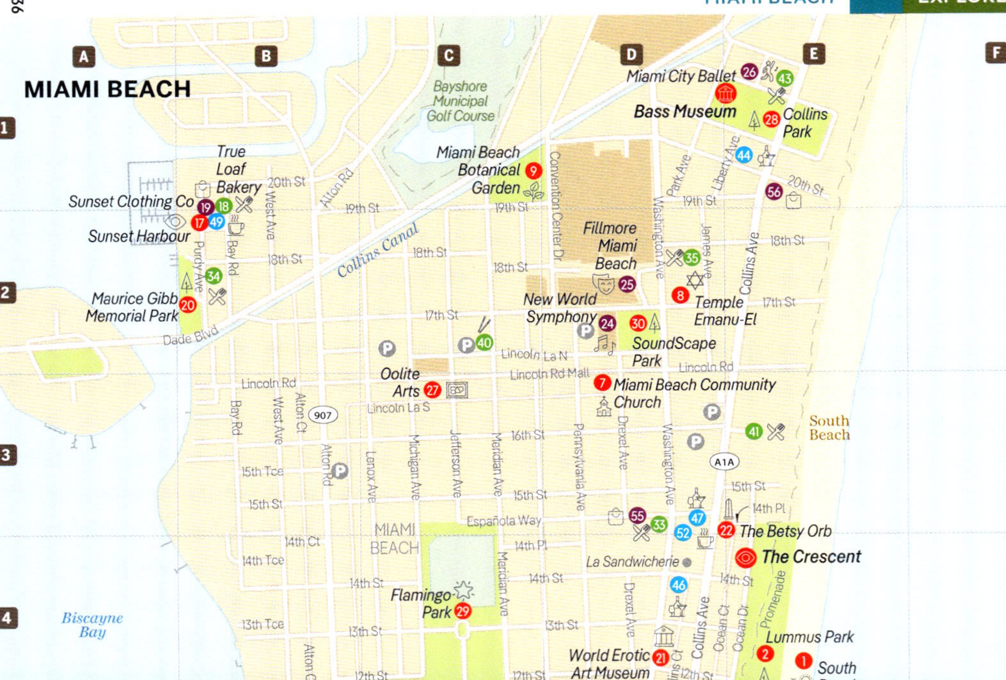
MIAMI BEACH
Bayshore Municipal Golf Course
Miami Beach Botanical Garden 9
Miami City Ballet 26
43
Bass Museum
Collins Park 28
44
56
True Loaf Bakery
Sunset Clothing Co 19 18
17 49
Sunset Harbour
34
Maurice Gibb Memorial Park 20
Collins Canal
Fillmore Miami Beach 25
35
Temple Emanu-El 8
New World Symphony 24
30
SoundScape Park
40
Oolite Arts 27
Miami Beach Community Church 7
South Beach
41
55
33
47
52
The Betsy Orb 22
The Crescent
La Sandwicherie
46
Flamingo Park 29
World Erotic Art Museum 21
Lummus Park 2
South 1
MIAMI BEACH
Biscayne Bay
Dade Blvd
Alton Rd
West Ave
Bay Rd
Purdy Ave
20th St
19th St
18th St
17th St
16th St
15th St
15th Tce
14th Ct
14th Tce
14th St
14th Pl
13th Tce
13th St
12th St
Lincoln Rd
Lincoln Rd Mall
Lincoln La N
Lincoln La S
Alton Ct
907
Lenox Ave
Michigan Ave
Jefferson Ave
Meridian Ave
Pennsylvania Ave
Drexel Ave
Washington Ave
Convention Center Dr
Park Ave
Liberty Ave
James Ave
Collins Ave
Española Way
A1A
Ocean Ct
Ocean Dr
Promenade

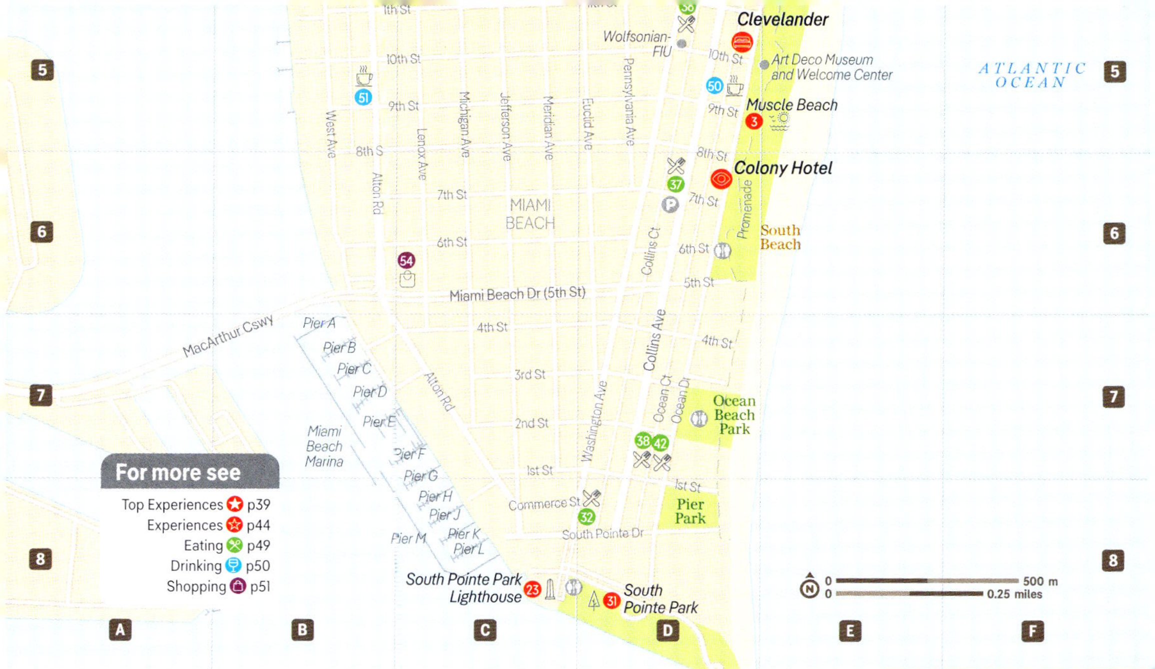

ATLANTIC OCEAN

Clevelander
Art Deco Museum and Welcome Center
Muscle Beach
Colony Hotel
Promenade
South Beach
Wolfsonian-FIU
Ocean Beach Park
Pier Park
South Pointe Park
South Pointe Park Lighthouse
Miami Beach Marina
MIAMI BEACH
MacArthur Cswy

Collins Ave
Collins Ct
Ocean Ct
Ocean Dr
Washington Ave
Pennsylvania Ave
Euclid Ave
Meridian Ave
Jefferson Ave
Michigan Ave
Lenox Ave
Alton Rd
West Ave
Miami Beach Dr (5th St)
Commerce St
South Pointe Dr
11th St
10th St
9th St
8th St
7th St
6th St
5th St
4th St
3rd St
2nd St
1st St

Pier A
Pier B
Pier C
Pier D
Pier E
Pier F
Pier G
Pier H
Pier J
Pier K
Pier L
Pier M

0 500 m
0 0.25 miles

A B C D E F
5 6 7 8

For more see

Top Experiences p39
Experiences p44
Eating p49
Drinking p50
Shopping p51

NORTH BEACH
1 km
0.5 miles
For more see
Top Experiences p39
Experiences p44
Eating p49
Drinking p50
Shopping p51
N Shore Dr
NORMANDY SHORES
S Shore Dr
Normandy Dr
Trouville Esplanade
71st St Bridge
71st St
Harding Ave
Collins Ave
North Beach
Altos Del Mar Sculpture Park
NORTH BEACH
JFK/79th St Cswy
NORTH BAY VILLAGE
Biscayne Bay
W 63rd St
La Gorce Country Club
A1A
La Gorce Dr
Pine Tree Dr
Indian Creek
ATLANTIC OCEAN
Alton Rd
Dade Blvd
MID-BEACH
907
Indian Creek Dr
41st St/Arthur Godfrey Rd
See Enlargement
195
Julia Tuttle Cswy
N Chase Ave
Sheridan Ave
Pine Tree Dr
South Beach
Sunset Islands
N Bay Rd
Alton Rd
Bayshore Municipal Golf Course
W 28th St
BAYSHORE
36 St
Faena District
35 St
BAYSHORE
Faena Bazaar
34 St
Faena Forum
Flamingo Dr
32nd St
Faena Hotel Miami Beach
Indian Creek
Indian Creek Dr
MID-BEACH
30 St
South Beach
Miami Beach Boardwalk
29th St
28th St
Collins Ave
100 m

★ TOP EXPERIENCE

Bass Museum

A fusion of history and contemporary art, all a stone's throw from the ocean, the Bass Museum *(thebass.org; adult/youth $15/8)* brings a bold and creative edge to the neighborhood. Housed in a prior 1930s library, its modern expansion blends seamlessly with the past. Inside, expect the most cutting-edge exhibitions, masterworks and a fresh perspective on local and global art alike.

MAP P36 **E1**

A Hub for Contemporary Art

The Bass is Miami Beach's premier contemporary art museum, known for its daring exhibitions, some of which spill into nearby Collins Park (p48). Since its founding in 1964, it has evolved into a space that showcases both emerging and established artists. The museum has hosted works by international heavyweights like El Anatsui, Isaac Julien and Piotr Uklański, ensuring a mix of global influence and Miami's own artistic energy.

Notable Exhibitions

Exhibitions at The Bass push boundaries and spark conversation. Examples among oh-so-many: Ellen Harvey's *The Nudist Museum* transformed gallery walls into a panorama of recreated classical nudes. In 2023 *Nam June Paik: The Miami Years* celebrated the pioneering video artist's influence. Ugo Rondinone's *good evening beautiful blue* turned a portion of the space into a dreamlike, meditative escape. Meanwhile, Sylvie Fleury's neon piece *Eternity Now* ever-beams from the museum's facade, an ongoing reminder of The Bass' forward-thinking.

Beyond the Galleries

The museum extends far beyond its walls with engaging talks, hands-on workshops and an ever-evolving outdoor sculpture park in Collins Park.

PLANNING TIP

For those seeking a bargain, the museum offers free admission every third Thursday of the month from 6 to 9pm. The last Sunday of the month is Family Day, with free admission for kids and caregivers.

Scan this QR code to book your visit and gauge ticketing options.

★ TOP EXPERIENCE

Art Deco Historic District

The world-famous Art Deco Historic District is pure exuberance: architecture of bold lines, whimsical tropical motifs and a color palette that evokes the beauty of Miami's landscape. Among the 800 deco buildings listed on the National Register of Historic Places, each design is different, and it's hard not to be captivated when strolling among these restored beauties from a bygone era.

MAP **P36**

PLANNING TIP
Go early in the day when crowds are thinnest and the light is best for taking pictures. Check out excellent deco exhibitions at the nearby Art Deco Museum and Welcome Center (p43) and Wolfsonian-FIU (p43).

Scan the QR code to book a guided Art Deco Walking Tour

A Bold New Beginning

In the early 20th century, Miami Beach was little more than a scrubby barrier island, slowly being shaped into a resort destination by a handful of ambitious developers. But in 1926 a devastating hurricane tore through South Florida, leveling much of the area. As the city began to rebuild, a new architectural movement was taking the world by storm: Art Deco. Inspired by the 1925 Exposition Internationale des Arts Décoratifs et Industriels Modernes in Paris, Miami Beach developers embraced the style, constructing hundreds of striking hotels throughout the 1930s to accommodate a growing wave of middle-class tourists.

The Art Deco Aesthetic

The Art Deco movement embodied the sleek, forward-thinking spirit of the late 1920s and 1930s. Influenced by automobiles, cruise ships and the age of industry, its defining features included bold vertical and horizontal lines, geometric patterns and streamlined curves. Miami Beach architects added a local twist, incorporating tropical motifs – flamingos, palm trees, waves and seashells among them – giving rise to a distinctive 'Tropical Deco'

MATTARISTUDIO/SHUTTERSTOCK

style. Practicality also played a role in the design: signature 'eyebrow' overhangs jutted over windows, shading interiors from the relentless South Florida sunshine while preserving views of the street below.

Where to See It

Nowhere is Miami Beach's Art Deco heritage more vividly displayed than along Ocean Dr, particularly between 11th and 14th Sts. Here, pastel-hued hotels with neon-lit facades transport visitors straight back to the city's prior heyday. The **Colony Hotel**, the curved corner of **The Crescent** (pictured) and the porthole windows of the **Clevelander** all showcase the defining playful elegance of this architectural era.

QUICK BREAK

Stop in for sandwiches and a cold drink at neighborhood-favorite **La Sandwicherie**. Complete the journey into the past with a meal at the **11th Street Diner** (p49), set in a 1940s train car.

Walk Miami Beach

Spend a morning walking around South Beach to admire the famous Art Deco Historic District, where the facades' sleek lines mixed with whimsical homages to tropical paradise make up the world's largest collection of 1920s and 1930s art deco buildings. Add some sure-to-greet-you thumpin' tunes, people-watching heaven and you're basically strolling through peak Miami.

START	END	LENGTH
Art Deco Museum	Wolfsonian-FIU	1.9 miles, 4 hrs

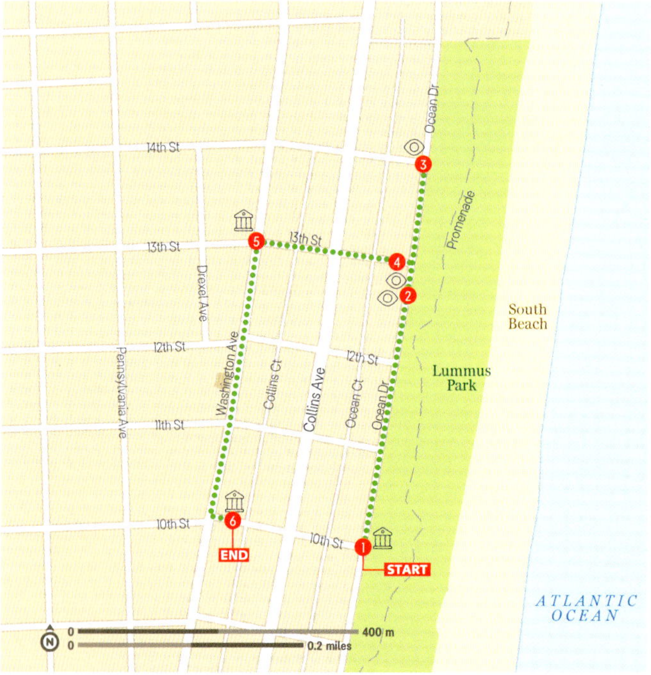

1 Art Deco Intro

Start at the **Art Deco Museum and Welcome Center** *(mdpl.org)*, where exhibits highlight the movement's bold geometric shapes, pastel colors and nautical influences. Learn how Miami Beach developed its signature tropical deco style and see original architectural drawings, vintage photos and period furniture. Join a guided walking tour or explore on your own.

2 Ocean Drive Stroll

Head north along Ocean Dr between 12th and 14th Sts, where some of the city's most iconic art deco hotels stand. **The Leslie** (1937) features a bright yellow facade and classic boxy shape, with cantilevered 'eyebrows' providing shade without blocking ocean views. At night, the bulk of Ocean Dr transforms into a neon wonderland, its pastel buildings glowing in blues, pinks and greens.

3 A Mid-Walk Haven

At 14th St step inside the **Winter Haven Hotel** to admire its polished terrazzo floors, a deco hallmark made of colorful stone chips set in mortar. The lobby's curved staircase and pastel hues maintain the building's 1930s elegance. After dark, cross into Lummus Park for a stunning shot of Ocean Dr's neon-lit hotels.

4 Hotel Hot Spots

Strolling by a portion of Lummus Park – perhaps you'll see bodybuilders flexing on the sands – you'll arrive at the **Carlyle**. Its modernist styling and strong vertical lines have been a Hollywood favorite, appearing in *Scarface* and *The Birdcage*. Venturing west off of Ocean Dr, the Cardozo Hotel (1939), designed by Henry Hohauser, stands out for its rounded corners and porthole windows, giving it a sleek, ocean-liner look. Now owned by Gloria and Emilio Estefan, it retains its deco charm with updated interiors.

5 Going Postal

From Ocean Drive, head inland on 13th St to Washington Ave, stopping at the **post office** on the corner. Built in 1937 it blends art deco with 'stripped classical' elements, creating a clean, geometric look. Inside, admire the period sunburst lighting fixture and streamlined aluminum details.

6 A Grand Finale

End your tour at the **Wolfsonian-FIU** *(wolfsonian.org)*, once the Washington Storage Company, where wealthy snowbirds stashed their valuables in the 1930s. Now a design museum it showcases art deco furniture, propaganda posters and industrial design. Its fortress-like facade contrasts with Ocean Dr's pastels, making it a fitting final stop on your deco journey.

EXPERIENCES

Strut & Sunbathe in South Beach

BEACHES

MAP: 1 P36 E4

When it comes to sun, sand and surf, Miami Beach covers all the bases – and with a different vibe to enjoy depending on where you choose to unfurl your beach towel.

South Beach is without a doubt the section of sand most people think of when they hear the words 'Miami Beach,' but there's far more coast to saunter along out here. Unless otherwise noted, the numbered streets here all extend off Collins Ave (A1A), which runs north and south parallel to the beach itself.

One of the liveliest areas along the strip is **Lummus Park** (MAP: 2 P36 E4; *miamibeachfl.gov; free*), a prime stretch of greenery between Ocean Dr and the beach. Joggers, skaters and sunbathers flock here to soak in the South Beach scene. Just steps away, fitness enthusiasts can get their pump on at **Muscle Beach** (MAP: 3 P36 E5; *instagram.com/musclebeachsouthbeach; free*), a famous outdoor gym where bodybuilders and casual fitness buffs show off their strength against a backdrop of swaying palms and neon-lit art deco hotels.

Saunter & Chill in Mid-Beach & North Beach

BEACHES

MAP: 4 P38 B5

Mid-Beach encompasses the beaches from 23rd to 63rd Sts. (Numbered streets extend off Collins Ave, which runs north–south, parallel to the beach itself.) It's not like the crowds out here stop preening and showing off – this is still model/influencer territory – but at least some of those influencers are past the 'post TikToks of my night at the club' phase and are moving into the 'boost reels of my growing family' end of the algorithm pool.

On the bayside of the beach is North Bay Rd, where you can see (well, glimpse over the walls) some of the area's largest mansions. This area includes the official **Miami Beach Boardwalk** (*miamibeachboardwalk.com, free*), which runs between 21st and 46th Sts, where Orthodox Jews often mix with social-media mavens.

Find Nature and Nudity in North Beach

BEACHES

MAP: 5 P38 D1

North Beach extends from 63rd St to 87th Tce, and the beaches here are smaller and more family-friendly, although this is also where you'll find **Haulover Beach Park** (MAP: 6 P38 C1), which is 4.5 miles north of 71st St. The northern section of this beach park is clothing optional and has been popular with naturists since the 1990s.

Say Your Prayers

CHURCHES

Few people might put 'Miami Beach' and 'quiet, worshipful reflection' in the same trip itinerary, let alone sentence, but guess what? There are some cool worship spaces out here. In rather sharp and refreshing contrast to the uber-modern structures muscling their way into the art deco design of South Beach, the **Miami Beach Community Church** (MAP: 7 P36 D3; *miamibeachcommunitychurch.com*) puts one in mind of an old Spanish mission – elegantly understated in an area where overstatement is the general philosophy. Built in 1921 this is the oldest church sanctuary in Miami Beach and it has a history of progressive politics, including ordaining African Americans and recognizing same-sex marriage. Sunday worship services are at 10:30am.

A quarter mile away is the smooth dome and sleek, almost aerodynamic profile of **Temple Emanu-El** (MAP: 8 P36 D2; *tesobe.org*), established in 1938. The design may seem deco-esque, but it's more Byzantine and Moorish in its influences, although elements of deco fit that rubric too. Shabbat services are on Friday at 6pm and Saturday at 10am.

Trade the Beach for Garden Scapes

GARDENS

Tucked away just steps from the buzz of South Beach, **Miami Beach Botanical Garden** (MAP: 9 P36 C1; *mbgarden.org; free*) is a lush, 2.6-acre retreat brimming with tropical flora, Japanese-inspired serenity and a refreshing escape from the city's energy. Operated by the Miami Beach Garden Conservancy, this hidden gem is a feast for the senses, where winding pathways lead past towering palms and a picturesque pond dotted with koi fish. Don't miss the butterfly garden, where native pollinators flit between colorful blossoms, or the edible garden, where tropical fruits and herbs flourish.

For another nature-filled respite, head to the **Altos Del Mar Sculpture Park** (MAP: 10 P38 D1; *free*), Miami Beach's only oceanfront green space blending art with tropical vibes. This seaside haven has large-scale contemporary sculptures against a backdrop of native dune vegetation.

MIAMI'S LITTLE ISRAEL

The center of gravity for American Jews is New York or Los Angeles, but you should also visit Miami Beach, specifically the area around Arthur Godfrey Rd (41st St) and Harding Ave between 91st and 96th Sts in Surfside. There's a unique cross-section of Jews here, from Northeast transplants to immigrants from former Soviet states to native-born 'Jewbans' (descendants of Jews and Cubans). Just as the Jewish population has shaped Miami Beach, so has the beach shaped them – you can eat lox y arroz con moros (salmon with rice and beans), and while Orthodox men don yarmulkes and women wear headscarves, many have nice tans and flashy SUVs.

Dive into a Beachy District
HISTORIC DISTRICT

The area of Mid-Beach from 32nd St to 36th St, known as the **Faena District** (MAP: 11 P38 B3; *faena.com; free*), was named for an Argentine businessman and developer, and is Miami Beach's answer to Wynwood. Spend a morning exploring this design-focused district, where urban character grows out of the intersection of the arts and attached commercial retail. The area is anchored by the **Faena Forum** (MAP: 12 P38 B4), an architectural dream that hosts performances, exhibitions, lectures and other events in a circular Rem Koolhaas–designed building.

Nearby is **Faena Hotel Miami Beach** (MAP: 13 P38 B4), characterized by heavy use of animal-print fabrics and coral and seashell decorative touches. Damien Hirst's iconic *Mammoth Garden* sculpture here is a timeless social media darling. And each room has butler service, because this is Miami, after all. Finally, high-end shoppers should check out **Faena Bazaar** (MAP: 14 P38 B3). Housed inside a historic hotel, it has four floors of expensive homewares and furniture for visitors who have lots of space in their checked bags.

Park it at a Park
PARKS

If you're looking to get outdoors in that sweet Miami tropical weather, the northern stretches of Miami Beach have you covered. With a playground, green fields, a hardwood hammock, a mangrove forest and views of the Oleta River, 249-acre **Greynolds Park** (MAP: 15 P38 C1) is a nice spot to savor the fresh air and let the kids run around.

The big outdoor attraction around here is **Oleta River State Park** (MAP: 16 P38 C1; *floridastateparks.org/OletaRiver; $6 per vehicle for up to 8 people*). At almost 1000 acres, it's the largest urban park in the state and one of the best places in Miami to escape the maddening crowds. Boat out to the local mangrove island, watch the eagles fly by or just chill on the pretension-free beach. How to access the aforementioned mangroves and inlets? An onsite outfitter offers both guided and self-directed adventures. You can rent kayaks, canoes, stand-up paddleboards and mountain bikes for exploring this stretch of North Biscayne Bay on your own.

Bounce to the Bayfront
NEIGHBORHOOD

Away from Ocean Dr and close to Lincoln Rd, palm-lined promenades and a bayfront shopping enclave draw a mix of local residents and savvy travelers who are less into flash, clubs and couture, and more attracted to indie stores, galleries, outdoor cafes and bakeries. All those and more give the **Sunset Harbour** (MAP: 17 P36 A2) neighborhood on the bay side of Miami Beach plenty of character.

Start the day with fresh pastries at **True Loaf Bakery** (MAP: 18 P36

B1; *trueloafbakery.square.site*). This well-regarded bakery is a bread-box-sized space where you can pick up heavenly croissants, tarts and kouign amann (Breton-style butter cake that is simply to die for).

Just around the block, **Sunset Clothing Co** (MAP: 19 P36 **B1**; *instagram.com/sunsetclothingco*) is a great little fashion boutique for stylish gear that won't cost a fortune (though it isn't cheap either). You'll find well-made shirts, soft cotton T-shirts, lace-up canvas shoes, nicely fitting denim (including vintage Levi's), warm sweaters (not that you need them here) and other casual gear.

Soak in the Sailboats

PARK

MAP: 20 P36 **B2**

Maurice Gibb Memorial Park is a five-minute walk away from Bayfront Park. This small palm-fringed green space overlooking the water has a playground, benches and grassy areas. It's a favorite destination for dog walkers, runners and families with kids. Against a backdrop of bobbing sailboats and the Venetian Causeway, it's worth stopping by to admire the view.

Catch a Big-Time or Local Show

PERFORMING ARTS

For lovers of the performing arts who prefer to bide most of their time out at the beach, there's no need to cross a bridge to Downtown Miami to get your cultural fill. You may want to begin by dipping your toes into the arts at the Frank Gehry–designed New World Center, home to the **New World Symphony** (MAP: 24 P36 **D2**; *nws.edu*) and the premier concert hall in Miami Beach. Here, scores

BEST OFFBEAT ART EXPERIENCES

World Erotic Art Museum

MAP: 21 P36 **D4**

(WEAM) A staggering collection of erotica including ancient sex manuals, explicit pre-Columbian sculptures, and works by Picasso and Rembrandt.

The Betsy Orb

MAP: 22 P36 **E3**

Near the tree-lined, pedestrian promenade of Española Way, look for this giant white beach-ball-like sculpture squashed into an alley between Ocean Dr and Collins Ave.

Poetry Rail

MAP: see 22 P36 **E3**

Right near the Orb, this metal wall is etched with the words of 12 poets, paying tribute to Miami's multicultural population and unique geography.

South Pointe Park Lighthouse

MAP: 23 P36 **C8**

Located in South Pointe Park, this 55ft-tall lighthouse artwork by German artist Tobias Rehberger is made of aluminum and frosted glass.

of young musicians are on fellowships that last three years, and a year-round event calendar hosts classical concerts, dance and much more. At the adjacent SoundScape Park, free WallCast concerts and movie screenings take place under the stars.

In a historic art deco space, the **Fillmore Miami Beach** (MAP: 25 P36 D2; *fillmore-miami.com*) at the Jackie Gleason Theater hosts comedians, ballet troupes, singer-songwriters and more. And the **Miami City Ballet** (MAP: 26 P36 E1; *miamicityballet.org*) is also at home in Miami Beach at the 63,000-square-foot Ophelia & Juan Js. Roca Center, which hosts regular performances by the troupe, one of the most renowned ballet companies in the US.

BEST URBAN SPACES

Lummus Park (p44)
MAP: see 2 P36 E4
Spanning a 10-block stretch of South Beach, with the Atlantic Ocean on one side and Ocean Dr on the other.

Collins Park
MAP: 28 P36 E1
Relax in this small green space with manicured lawns and a giant baobab tree, nestled between the Holocaust Memorial and the beach.

Flamingo Park
MAP: 29 P36 C4
Sports lovers flock here for courts and fields catering to tennis, handball, racquetball, basketball, soccer and more.

SoundScape Park
MAP: 30 P36 D2
A 2.5-acre urban park next to the New World Center, hosting family-friendly films and WallCast concerts.

South Pointe Park
MAP: 31 P36 D8
Gorgeous green space and beach on the southern tip of Miami Beach with a playground, walking trails and picnic areas.

Get Artsy at Oolite Arts

ARTS

MAP: 27 P36 C3

Once known as ArtCenter/South Florida South Beach, this exhibition space includes dozens of artists' studios, many of which are open to the public. Oolite Arts also offers a slate of sought-after residencies, reserved for artists who do not have major exposure, making this a good place to spot up-and-coming talent. Monthly rotating exhibitions keep the presentation fresh and pretty avant-garde.

Alongside the art there is a printshop on hand, open by appointment (email printshop@oolitearts.org), and the facility hosts virtual and in-person arts classes.

Best Places for...

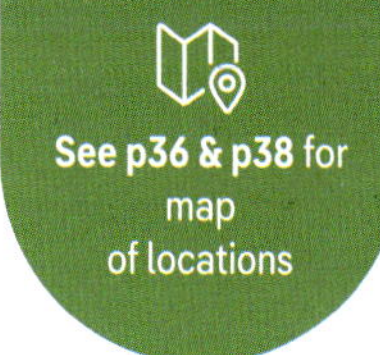

$ Budget $$ Midrange $$$ Top End

Eating

Seafood

Joe's Stone Crab $$$
32 P36 D8
Try the seasonal and sustainable crab claws local to Florida at this South Beach staple (mustard sauce obligatory). *joesstonecrab.com, 5pm-10pm Mon & Tue, 11:30am-10pm Wed, Thu & Sun, to 11pm Fri & Sat*

Mercato della Pescheria Miami Beach $$
33 P36 D3
Italian seafood market vibes in South Beach with flopping fresh fish and delicious steaks on the menu. *mercatodellapescheria.com, 11:30am-11:30pm Sun-Thu, to 12:30am Fri & Sat*

Stiltsville Fish Bar $$
34 P36 B2
Coconut shrimp, ceviche and red snapper all fly off the menu at this breezy restaurant with indoor and outdoor seating. *stiltsvillefishbar.com, noon-10pm Mon-Thu, to 11pm Fri, 11am-11pm Sat, to 10pm Sun*

Lobster Shack $$
35 P36 D2
With a beachfront and Lincoln Rd location, this spot reels them in for piled-high lobster rolls made with the good stuff from Maine. *lobstershack-miami.com, 11am-midnight*

Diners

11th Street Diner $$
36 P36 D5
Dine on great shrimp and grits, and sandwiches in a gleaming retro aluminum Pullman car that was imported in 1992 from Wilkes-Barre, PA. *eleventhstreetdiner.com, 7:30am-midnight Sun-Thu, 24hr Fri & Sat*

Puerto Sagua $
37 P36 D6
This beloved Cuban diner has been slinging *ropa vieja* (Cuban-style shredded beef in tomato sauce; in huge portions) since 1962. *puertosagua.org, 7am-11pm*

Big Pink $
38 P36 D7
Come for gourmet comfort food and retro vibes where the daily specials are served on a stainless-steel tray. *mylesrestaurantgroup.com/big-pink/, 8am-midnight*

Arlen Beach Restaurant $
39 P38 D3
American breakfasts, authentic Cuban cuisine, bagels and lox, empanadas and pancakes tick a lot of boxes in one stop. *arlenbeachrestaurant.com, 9:30am-9pm Sun & Mon, to 3pm Tue, 10am-9pm Wed & Thu, 9:30am-10pm Fri & Sat*

Date Night

MILA $$$
40 P36 C2
With an omakase-style rooftop bar, this swanky four-concept restaurant takes guests on a culinary odyssey from the Mediterranean to Japan. *mila-miami.com, hours vary*

Mac's Club Deuce

RAO's $$$

41 P36 **E3**

Upscale Italian restaurant in the Loews Miami Beach Hotel known for its raw bar, antipasti courses and southern Neapolitan cuisine. *raosonmiami beach.com, 5:30pm-10pm Sun-Thu, to 11pm Fri & Sat*

Forte dei Marmi $$$

42 P36 **D7**

Helmed by a two-Michelin-star chef, this coastal Italian restaurant occupies a Mediterranean-revival building designed to conjure a Tuscan villa. *fdmmiami.com, hours vary*

Baires Grill $$

43 P36 **E1**

Authentic Argentinean *parrillada* (barbecue) for two steals the show alongside *milanesas* (veal schnitzels) just like in Buenos Aires. *bairesgrill. com,* noon-*11pm Sun-Thu, to 11:30pm Fri & Sat*

Drinking

Cocktail Bars

Sweet Liberty

44 P36 **E1**

Friendly bartenders whip up excellent cocktails amid flickering candles and a long wooden bar. *mysweetliberty.com, 4pm-4am*

Broken Shaker

45 P38 **A5**

This well-equipped bar produces expert cocktails, which are mostly consumed in the beautiful, softly lit garden. *freehandhotels. com, 5pm-2am*

Bars

Mac's Club Deuce

46 P36 **D4**

The oldest bar in Miami Beach, the Deuce is a seedy neighborhood dive par excellence. *macsclub-deuce.com, 8am-5am*

Kill Your Idol

47 P36 **D3**

This lovable hipster spot has graffiti and shelves full of retro bric-à-brac covering the walls. *8pm-5am*

Twist

see 36 P36 **D5**

DJs and drag queens mean there's never a dull moment at this two-story gay club with seven different bars. *twistsobe.com, 3pm-5am*

Bob's Your Uncle

48 P38 **C2**

Casual and friendly neighborhood bar with classic cocktails, cold beer, old games, plenty of seating and some of Miami Beach's most chilled-out vibes. *bobsyourunclemiami.com, 3pm-3am*

Coffee Shops

Panther Coffee

49 P36 **B2**

Specialty coffee shop in Sunset Harbour known for small-batch roasting and industrial-chic decor. *panthercoffee.com, 7am-5pm*

Shepherd Artisan Coffee

50 P36 **D5**

Collins Ave favorite for beautiful morning pastries and strong brews with breakfast served all day. *shepherdartisan.com, 7am-8pm*

Malua Cozy Coffee

51 P36 **B5**

Come for an Oreo latte or a more standard espresso drink and don't miss the empanadas at this special spot. *maluacozycoffee.com, 7am-4pm Mon-Fri, 8am-3pm Sat & Sun*

Cortadito Coffee House

52 P36 **D4**

With locations on Lincoln Rd and Washington Ave, this is the spot for the legendary strong and sugary Cuban coffee shots. *cortaditocoffee-house.com, 7am-10pm*

Shopping

All in One

Bal Harbour Shops

53 P38 **C1**

The pinnacle of luxury shopping in Miami Beach, this open-air mall is home to designer boutiques like Chanel, Gucci and Prada, all surrounded by lush tropical landscaping. *balharbourshops.com, 11am-10pm Mon-Sat, noon-6pm Sun*

Fifth and Alton

54 P36 **C6**

This multilevel shopping center has essentials like Target, Publix and Best Buy, making it a convenient stop for both visitors and locals in need of everyday goods. *8am-10pm*

Española Way

55 P36 **D3**

A charming pedestrian street lined with boutique shops with artisanal goods and unique souvenirs, offering a mix of European flair and Miami's vibrant culture. *visitespanolaway.com, 10am-11pm*

Trendy

Kith Miami Beach

56 P36 **E1**

A sleek concept store blending high-end streetwear, sneakers and lifestyle goods. Expect limited-edition drops and a stylish crowd. *kith.com, 11am-8pm*

See p70
for eating,
drinking and
shopping
listings

Explore
Downtown Miami

Downtown Miami and Brickell are where history meets modern luxury. Once a trading post and a hub for Miami's early development, the area grew into the city's financial core. Brickell, once lined with grand mansions, transformed into the 'Wall Street of the South,' its skyline now dominated by glassy high-rises. Downtown, once sleepy after business hours, has evolved into a vibrant mix of arts, entertainment and upscale living hubs. Today, soaring condos, rooftop bars and waterfront parks define the scene, blending the Miami grit of yesteryear with new-world glamour.

Getting Around

Metromover

The Metromover is a free, automated people mover serving Downtown Miami and Brickell. With three loops – Omni, Brickell and Inner – it provides easy access to major attractions, hotels and connecting transit hubs.

Trolleys

Miami's free trolley system runs multiple routes through Downtown and Brickell, connecting core destinations like Bayside Marketplace, Brickell City Centre and museums.

Walking

Downtown Miami and Brickell are highly walkable, with generally pedestrian-friendly streets, riverwalks and bridges linking major hotels, shopping destinations and entertainment clusters.

THE BEST

MIAMI NIGHTCLUB E11EVEN Miami (p69)

PLACE TO TAKE KIDS Phillip & Patricia Frost Museum of Science (p67)

VENUE TO CATCH A SHOW Adrienne Arsht Center for the Performing Arts (p58)

SPOT FOR A BAYSIDE STROLL Bayfront Park (p60)

SHOPPING UTOPIA Brickell City Centre (p71)

Brickell
MDV EDWARDS/SHUTTERSTOCK

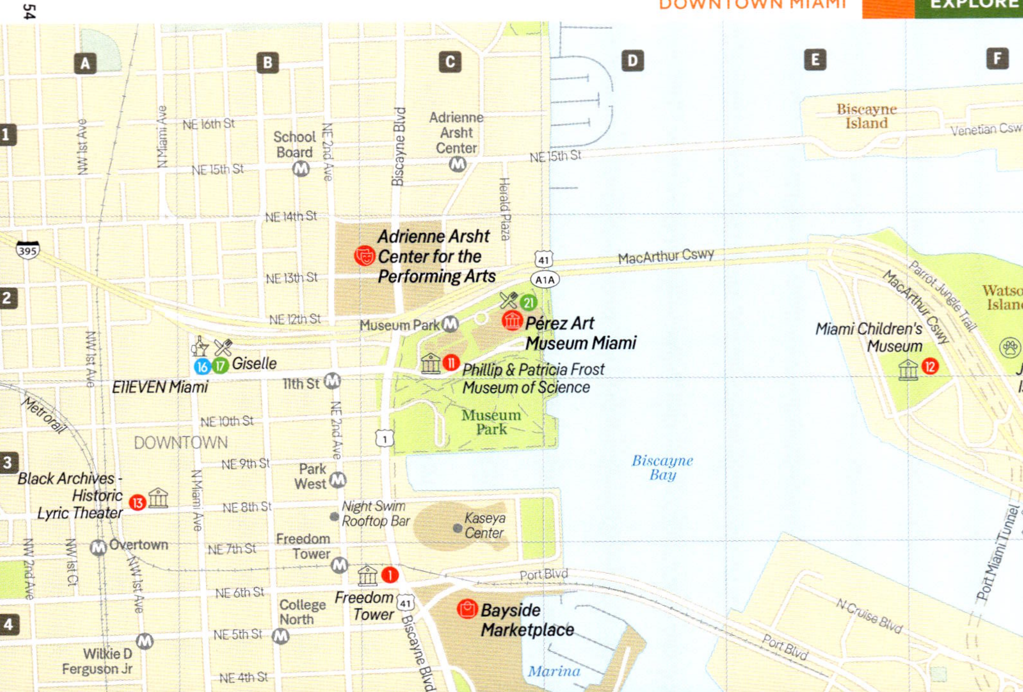
Biscayne Island
Venetian Cswy
Adrienne Arsht Center
School Board
NE 16th St
NE 15th St
NE 14th St
NE 13th St
NE 12th St
NE 2nd Ave
Biscayne Blvd
Herald Plaza
N Miami Ave
NW 1st Ave
Adrienne Arsht Center for the Performing Arts
MacArthur Cswy
Parrot Jungle Trail
Watson Island
Miami Children's Museum
Jungle Island
Museum Park
Pérez Art Museum Miami
Phillip & Patricia Frost Museum of Science
Museum Park
Giselle
EllEVEN Miami
11th St
NE 10th St
DOWNTOWN
Metrorail
Black Archives - Historic Lyric Theater
NE 9th St
Park West
NE 8th St
Night Swim Rooftop Bar
Kaseya Center
Biscayne Bay
Overtown
NE 7th St
Freedom Tower
Port Blvd
Port Miami Tunnel
NE 6th St
College North
Freedom Tower
Bayside Marketplace
NE 5th St
Wilkie D Ferguson Jr
NE 4th St
Marina
N Cruise Blvd
Port Blvd
NW 2nd Ave
NW 1st Ct
NW 1st Ave

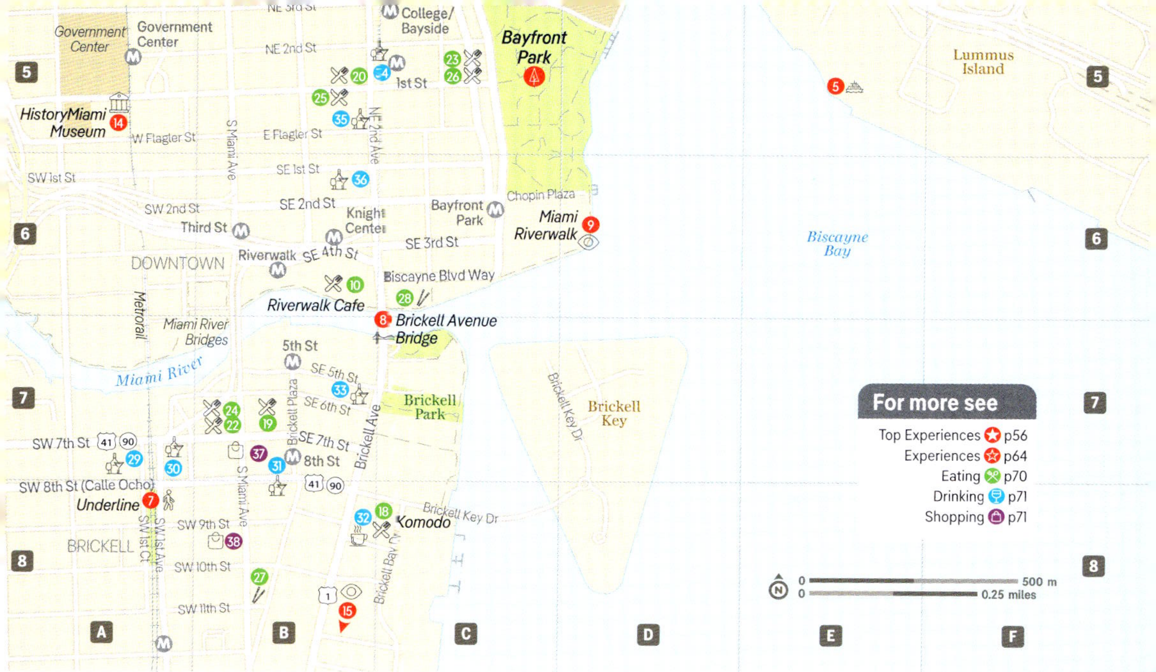

For more see

Top Experiences p56
Experiences p64
Eating p70
Drinking p71
Shopping p71

0 500 m
0 0.25 miles

A B C D E F
5 6 7 8

Lummus Island
5
Biscayne Bay
Bayfront Park
Chopin Plaza
9 Miami Riverwalk
Brickell Key
Brickell Key Dr
College/Bayside
1st St
NE 3rd St
NE 2nd St
NE 2nd Ave
E Flagler St
SE 1st St
SE 2nd St
Bayfront Park
Knight Center
SE 3rd St
Biscayne Blvd Way
Riverwalk
SE 4th St
Riverwalk Cafe
8 Brickell Avenue Bridge
5th St
SE 5th St
SE 6th St
SE 7th St
8th St
Brickell Plaza
Brickell Ave
Brickell Park
Brickell Key Dr
Komodo
Brickell Bay Dr
15
Government Center
HistoryMiami Museum 14
W Flagler St
SW 1st St
SW 2nd St
Third St
S Miami Ave
DOWNTOWN
Miami River Bridges
Miami River
Metrorail
SW 7th St
SW 8th St (Calle Ocho)
Underline 7
SW 1st Ave
SW 1st Ct
SW 9th St
SW 10th St
SW 11th St
BRICKELL
41 90 1
4 20 23 25 26 35 36 10 28 33 19 24 22 37 31 30 29 18 32 38 27

★ TOP EXPERIENCE

Pérez Art Museum Miami

Miami has no shortage of first-rate galleries and intriguing museums. The Pérez Art Museum Miami *(pamm.org; adult/youth $18/14)*, though, is in a category of its own. This gorgeous building, known as PAMM locally, was designed by Pritzker Prize–winning architecture firm Herzog & de Meuron. The world-class contemporary art looks all the more impressive viewed in these light-filled galleries on the edge of Biscayne Bay.

MAP P54 **C2**

PLANNING TIP
PAMM offers free admission on the first Thursday and second Saturday of each month. It's free the first full weekend of the month for Bank of America cardholders, through the Museums on Us program.

Scan this QR code to find out what's on now at PAMM.

The Building Itself

PAMM is an architectural landmark that merges tropical elements with modern design. Opened in 2013 the 200,000-square-foot museum sits on an elevated platform, offering views of Biscayne Bay. The design incorporates South Florida's environment, with slender columns under its canopy resembling mangrove roots and a facade combining glass, wood and concrete. The hanging gardens originally contained native plants sustained by rainwater. Though replaced with artificial greenery in 2023 due to upkeep challenges, they remain a defining visual element. The museum's design ensures a seamless connection between indoor and outdoor spaces, inviting visitors to experience Miami's tropical setting while engaging with contemporary art.

All That Awaits Inside

PAMM presents contemporary art exhibitions featuring both established and emerging artists. The permanent collection rotates regularly, drawing from works spanning the last 80 years. Temporary exhibitions have showcased artists such as Ai Weiwei, Julio Le Parc and Robert Rauschenberg. The museum's open galleries allow for an intuitive and immersive experience. Visitors can find themselves

MARIAKRAY/SDHUTTERSTOCK

lingering in the airy, light-filled spaces, where large windows frame striking views of the bay, integrating the outside world into the museum experience.

Well Beyond the Art

The museum's on-site cafe offers a place to pause, with a menu featuring locally inspired dishes and waterfront seating. Nearby Museum Park connects PAMM with the Phillip & Patricia Frost Museum of Science (p67), forming a cultural hub along the bay. The surrounding public spaces, with their lawns and walkways, serve as an extension of the museum itself, fostering a lively yet relaxed atmosphere where visitors unwind. The museum's waterfront terrace provides shaded seating, and Museum Park offers a quiet green space. Deck chairs and outdoor seating encourage visitors to take in the bay views, making PAMM as much a gathering place as a museum.

QUICK BREAK
Night Swim Rooftop Bar at the citizenM Miami Worldcenter isn't just open at night. It has stellar bites and sweeping city-meets-bay vistas.

★ TOP EXPERIENCE

Adrienne Arsht Center for the Performing Arts

Miami's cultural heartbeat, Adrienne Arsht Center for the Performing Arts *(arshtcenter.org)* stands among the world's great venues – Miami's answer to New York's Lincoln Center and Sydney's Opera House. This complex is a cornerstone of the Miami arts scene, hosting ballet, opera, Broadway tours and cutting-edge theater.

MAP P54 **C2**

PLANNING TIP
Free guided tours are offered at noon on Mondays and Saturdays. You'll want to call ahead to ensure they're running. Tours are approximately 90 minutes.

Scan this QR code to buy tickets online. The box office opens 90 minutes before showtime.

Creative Spaces Within

The Adrienne Arsht Center for the Performing Arts is a true testament to Miami's commitment to growing artistic spaces. The Ziff Ballet Opera House, seating 2400, is known for its horseshoe-shaped layout, ensuring impeccable sightlines for top-tier opera performances and more. Across the street and perhaps the broader center's gem, the Knight Concert Hall has three tiers and killer acoustics, built to amplify even the subtlest notes. The Carnival Studio Theater, an adaptable 300-seat space, supports smaller productions and experimental works.

The Epicenter of a Changing Skyline

When the Arsht Center opened in 2006, it was a cultural island in an undeveloped part of Downtown. Today it sits at the crossroads of an evolving cityscape. From its upper-level viewpoints you can see a skyline that has changed dramatically over the years, with new high-rises reflecting Miami's economic and cultural growth just outside. The center's presence helped spur development in the surrounding neighborhood, solidifying its role as more than a theater – it is a cornerstone of Miami's transformation.

FELIX MIZIOZNIKOV/SHUTTERSTOCK

A Center for All

More than just a performance venue, the Arsht Center has year-round public programs, educational outreach and community events that expand its reach beyond traditional theatergoers. Free concerts, dance workshops and artist talks provide an opportunity for locals and visitors to have access to the arts. The Arsht Center is also home to multiple resident companies, including the Florida Grand Opera and Miami City Ballet, ensuring an ever-changing lineup of performances. Regular collaborations with international artists and touring productions make it a cultural bridge connecting Miami to the global arts scene – you never know who or what may come next, but you know it will be great.

QUICK BREAK

Within a 10-minute walk of the Arsht Center is **Vice City Bean** a local coffee roaster and specialty coffee shop with a pastry selection.

★ TOP EXPERIENCE

Bayfront Park

Whereas Miami Beach's eastern edge is a sandy playground, Downtown Miami's includes a grassy, urban oasis. Bayfront Park (*bayfrontparkmiami.com*) offers sweeping views of Biscayne Bay's waters, the Miami skyline and the bustling Port of Miami. It's a prime spot for leisurely strolls, waterfront picnics and cultural experiences, including open-air concerts, free yoga sessions and sure, periodic trapeze classes.

MAP P54 **C5**

PLANNING TIP
Double-check the calendar of the **Kaseya Center** – home of the NBA's Miami Heat and mega-concerts year-round. The arena is just north of the park and an event could make a great pairing with your outing.

Scan this QR code for details on the park's next free yoga class.

Land at These Landmarks

Redesigned in the 1980s by renowned artist and landscape architect Isamu Noguchi, Bayfront Park fosters a welcoming atmosphere for visitors from all walks of life. The park is dotted with sculptures and memorials that add a layer of depth to its scenic beauty. In the southwest corner, the *Challenger Memorial* honors the astronauts lost in the 1986 space-shuttle disaster with a design that evokes both a DNA helix and the shuttle itself. Nearby the *Light Tower,* a 40ft abstract structure, nods to Japanese lanterns and moonlit Miami nights. The most playful of the bunch? *The Slide Mantra,* a twisting spiral of marble that doubles as a slide for kids.

Concerts &...High-Flying Thrills?

Live entertainment thrives at Bayfront Park. The Klipsch Amphitheater hosts major concerts with unbeatable waterfront views, while the Tina Hills Pavilion offers a more intimate venue with free springtime performances. Beyond the music, the park is also a hub for unique activities. Fitness lovers can stretch it out at free yoga classes, while daredevils can take to the skies with flying trapeze lessons at the park's dedicated trapeze school. For families, there's a well-equipped playground

PAPA BRAVO/SHUTTERSTOCK

to keep the little ones entertained between strolls along the bay. Each year, Bayfront Park transforms into the epicenter of some of Miami's biggest events, including the world-famous Ultra Music Festival and the city's largest New Year's Eve celebration, featuring fireworks over Biscayne Bay.

Shopping, Dining & Bayside Fun

Right next door, **Bayside Marketplace** is a lively extension of the Bayfront Park experience. This open-air shopping and entertainment complex offers everything from souvenir stalls to waterfront restaurants. Grab a Cuban sandwich at Havana 1957, sip a mojito at Mambo Café or hop on a speedboat tour for a thrilling ride through Biscayne Bay – congrats, you're officially Miami-ing to the max.

QUICK BREAK
Stroll two blocks west of the park to **Julia & Henry's**, a five-story food hall with 25 restaurants and three bars for quick, locally inspired satisfaction.

Walk Downtown Miami

Downtown Miami is constantly reinventing itself via construction and early adoption of whatever the world thinks is cool. If you want to have your finger on the pulse of what's on trend and also tread the city as locals do, this walk will lead you past the shiniest corners inhabited by Miami's relentlessly cool kids.

START	END	LENGTH
El Sitio Coffee Bar	Coyo Taco	2.5 miles; 4 hours

1 Breakfast & Coffee

Start your stroll on a mellow and authentic note with a great breakfast of Venezuelan street food and caffeine at **El Sitio Coffee Bar**. Menu highlights of this cozy yet hip spot include arepas, empanadas, cachapa (corn pancakes) and café con leche (coffee with milk) – the perfect fuel to get you geared up for a Miami stroll.

2 An Urban Green Space

This 32-acre urban oasis on Biscayne Bay is known to get rowdy within its large on-site music venue, but most days **Bayfront Park** (p60) is a serene escape for those looking for a way to unwind. The park has walking trails, playgrounds, picnic spaces and public art installations by Isamu Noguchi.

3 Walk the Walk

Along the Miami River lies a beautiful juxtaposition of urban development and natural wonders beneath the surface of its waters. Look up along the **Miami Riverwalk** (p66) and spot luxury high-rises that are iconic to the Downtown Miami skyline. Look down and you might spot a dolphin or manatee swimming by.

4 Over the River

Crossing the Miami River via the **Brickell Avenue Drawbridge** offers sweeping views of the Downtown skyline. The bridge is a great spot to snap some photos or check out the 17ft bronze statue by Cuban-born sculptor Manuel Carbonell of a Tequesta Indian warrior and his family, which sits atop the towering Pillar of History.

5 A Historic Site

Just east of Brickell Ave lies an archaeological oddity – the **Miami Circle National Historic Landmark** marks the site on which 24 holes forming a perfect circle in the limestone were uncovered. It is thought to be the only prehistoric permanent structure cut into bedrock ever found in the eastern United States.

6 Fall Under Line

Miami's newest way to stay active, the **Underline**, takes advantage of the space under the city's elevated Metrorail. Currently a half-mile portion is open to the public (with plans to expand to 10 miles) boasting an outdoor gym, a basketball court, game tables, a walking and biking trail, a butterfly garden and more.

7 Taco Bout It

A classic Miami spot to cool off and refuel is **Coyo Taco**. The Brickell location is conveniently located just off the Underline, making it the perfect wrap to a stroll. Indulge in Mexican-style street food, from tacos and burritos to fresh guacamole, or sip on strong margaritas.

EXPERIENCES

Glide Around on the Metromover

TRANSPORTATION

What's that train whirring overhead through some of Miami's densest real estate? The answer is the **Metromover** *(miamidade.gov; free)*, an elevated, electric monorail designed to provide mass transit and ease Downtown and Brickell traffic. While it hasn't solved South Florida's congestion (as any driver can attest), it remains a beloved rail system moving thousands through Downtown for free. It's also a cool way to see central Miami from above, given the city's skyscraper canyons (and again: it's free).

Opened in 1986 the Metromover has that retro-futuristic public works aesthetic. It features three loops – Omni, Inner and Brickell – spanning 4.4 miles and connecting major landmarks like Bayfront Park (p60), Kaseya Center (p60) and the Adrienne Arsht Center (p58). It also offers great views of the **Freedom Tower** (MAP: 1 P54 C4), modeled after the Giralda bell tower in Spain's Seville Cathedral. Trains run 5am to midnight every three minutes (even more frequently at rush hour), seven days a week.

Zip Around in a Speedboat

TRANSPORTATION

The Atlantic Ocean might be a causeway away from Downtown Miami, but you can still get out on the area's sparkling waterways from Downtown's shoreline by taking a boat tour with one of the companies operating out of Bayside Marketplace (p61). For a serious rush, **Thriller Miami Speedboat Adventures** *(thrillermiami.com, per person $45)* offers

Metromover

Miami Vice–style tours (Don Johnson sightings not guaranteed) aboard its fleet of three power catamarans. These 45-minute outings take you across Biscayne Bay and past the mansions of **Fisher Island** (MAP: 2 P54 **F3**) and **Star Island** (MAP: 3 P54 **F3**).

Island Queen Cruises *(islandqueencruises.com; adult/child $35/25)* offers a slower-paced, 90-minute sightseeing cruise on a private ship with an open upper deck and air-conditioned salon. The tour passes sites like **Millionaire's Row** (MAP: 4 P54 **F1**), Miami Beach and the **Port of Miami** (MAP: 5 P54 **E5**).

On both tours, it's impressive to catch sight of Downtown Miami's shoreline and skyscrapers from the turquoise waters, showcasing just how truly tropical the city is.

Monkey Around on Jungle Island

AMUSEMENT AREA

MAP: 6 P54 **F2**

Tucked on Watson Island, a blip on the radar between Downtown Miami and South Beach, **Jungle Island** *(jungleisland.com; adult/child $44/28)* is a South Florida landmark and eco-adventure park. It's the kind of attraction you'd really only expect to find in a place like Miami.

Those capybaras that have gone viral on social media lately? You'll find them living their next-best lives here, alongside a veritable Noah's Ark of other creatures, including tropical birds, alligators, chimps, lemurs, sloths and so much more. In short, Jungle Island is a good bit of smelly fun. It's one of those places kids (justifiably) beg to go, so just give up and prepare for some bright-feathered, bird-poop-scented enjoyment in this artificial, self-contained jungle.

Also on offer: rope bridges among the trees, a flight-generating wind tunnel, an escape room and Adventure Bay, with rock-climbing

UNDER THE TRACKS

Miami's Metrorail connects Downtown to residential neighborhoods, including Coral Gables and Coconut Grove. But it's what's beneath the Metrorail that we're focusing on here: the well-titled **Underline**, a planned $146-million, 10-mile-long linear park that will run underneath much of the Metrorail's tracks. The park is set to be completed in 2026, and the second phase, which runs from Brickell to Vizcaya Station, was unveiled in 2024. You'll find weekly community yoga classes staged on the Underline – because Miami law requires all public spaces to host yoga classes (kidding, sort of) – as well as an outdoor gym, a meditation garden, and, of course, a walking and biking path to explore.

MAP: 7 P54 **A8**

walls and kid-friendly bungee jumping. Do all of these activities cost a fair amount extra? You better believe it. You can even head out on a Treetop Trekking course here – South Florida's only aerial adventure park.

Meander Miami's Financial Heart NEIGHBORHOOD

Brickell *(brickell.com)* is perhaps the ritziest neighborhood in Miami (which is saying something). Located just south of Downtown, Brickell has a reputation as the financial heart of South Florida. That identity remains, but it's been glittered over by a glut of restaurants, bars and nightclubs.

The Miami River forms the northern border of Brickell, spanned by the lovely **Brickell Avenue Bridge** (MAP: 8 P54 **C7**), which sits between SE 4th St and SE 5th St. At the edge of the bridge is a bronze statue of a Tequesta (Native American) warrior aiming his arrow at the sky. The bridge itself is accented with reliefs that honor Miamians like Everglades conservationist Julia Tuttle. Walking here is the best way to see the sculptures and will also allow you to avoid one of the most confusing traffic patterns in Miami.

Worth a detour, **Brickell Key** is an island that is technically part of Brickell proper. It looks more like a floating porcupine, with glass towers for quills, than an island.

Stroll the Miami Riverwalk PROMENADE

The Tequesta Indians built the first human settlement here, where the Miami River meets Biscayne Bay. Over the centuries, the land has undergone a drastic transformation.

A walkway shapes itself around this vital geography, a shoreline promenade that follows the northern edge of the river as it bisects Downtown. It winds past high-rise condos and battered warehouses,

THE HISTORY OF BISCAYNE BOULEVARD

Designed in the 1920s to be Miami's most beautiful shopping street, Biscayne Blvd was opened to automobile traffic in 1927 and took off like a hot rod. In the 1950s Frank Sinatra, Sammy Davis Jr and Dean Martin were all said to have hung out along the Boulevard at the Vagabond Hotel, one of many motels once lining it. Miami's very evolution is reflected in the variety of buildings lining it, ranging from the Boom-era Freedom Tower to mid-1930s and 1940s art deco edifices to today's gleaming towers and offices housing consulates, consultancy firms and much more.

Miami Riverwalk

with a few small tugboats pulling along the glassy surface. Fisherfolk float in with their daily catch, while fancy yachts make their way in and out of the bay.

At night, you can see the Brickell skyline's lights up close and in person on the **Miami Riverwalk** (MAP: 9 P54 **D6**), and you can often spot manatees and dolphins frolicking in the middle of this unlikely bustling urban locale. Stop under the shade of tropical trees to admire the views.

For something cool to drink or a meal that blends American and Latin cuisine, pop into the **Riverwalk Cafe** (MAP: 10 P54 **B6**; *hyatt.com*) at the Hyatt Regency Miami.

Embark on a Quick Museum-Hop

MUSEUMS

Start at the **Phillip & Patricia Frost Museum of Science** (MAP: 11 P54 **C2**). Families love the 250-seat planetarium's immersive shows, while the three-level aquarium dazzles all ages, highlighting Florida's coral reefs and Everglades critters. Recent exhibits include the likes of *Feathers to the Stars*, tracing the evolution of flight from dinosaurs to space travel.

From here walk 15 minutes or hop on the Metromover to the **Miami Children's Museum** (MAP: 12 P54 **F2**). This interactive paradise lets kids play music, explore an undersea world and sketch on giant walls. On a given day, kids can be playing with construction blocks or messing with gravity.

Finally, take a 10-minute drive or ride to the **Black Archives - Historic Lyric Theater** (MAP: 13 P54 **A3**), a 1913 landmark that once hosted jazz legends like Duke Ellington. Today, it presents exhibitions on Miami's African American heritage. Check out *Visions of Freedom*, a deep dive into local civil rights history.

Hone In On Miami's History

MUSEUMS

Making sense of today's Miami means exploring South Florida's multifaceted and fascinating past. This land of escaped enslaved people, guerrilla Native Americans, gangsters, pirates, tourists and alligators has a unique history – and it takes a special place to capture that narrative.

A Smithsonian Affiliate, **HistoryMiami Museum** (MAP: 14 P54 **A5**; *historymiami.org, adult/child $15/8*), located in the Miami-Dade Cultural Center, does just that. It weaves together the stories of the region's successive population waves, from Native Americans to Nicaraguans.

Interactive exhibits showcase life among the Seminoles and Florida's early industries, like sponge diving. Other sections highlight the histories of Jewish and African American communities in South Beach, Cuban refugees – complete with a rustic homemade boat that survived the Florida crossing – and cultural expression in public spaces, from street art to protests and vehicle customizing.

Special tours and events run year-round, including themed family days like Cuban Carnival and historian-led cruises to **Stiltsville** (MAP: 15 P54 **B8**), a unique community built on stilts in the middle of Biscayne Bay.

'ELLIS ISLAND OF THE SOUTH'

Impossible to miss along Biscayne Blvd, the richly ornamented Freedom Tower, which was completed in 1925, is one of two surviving towers modeled after the Giralda bell tower in Spain's Seville Cathedral. As the 'Ellis Island of the South,' it served as an immigration processing center for almost half a million Cuban refugees in the 1960s. Placed on the National Register of Historic Places in 1979, the tower also houses the Miami Museum of Art & Design (MOAD), which features exhibits ranging from contemporary sculpture to historical photography. The tower and MOAD are scheduled to reopen to the public in 2025 with a re-imagined visitor experience in time for the tower's 100th anniversary.

Party 24/7 at E11EVEN

NIGHTLIFE

Miami's nightlife never sleeps, and nowhere embodies that better than **E11EVEN Miami** (MAP: 16 P54 **B2**; *11miami.com*). Open 24/7, this part-nightclub, part-cabaret, part-total-sensory-overload mega-club redefines after-dark entertainment. Just steps from Downtown's skyscrapers, it pulls in big-name DJs and A-list artists – Drake, Cardi B and Diplo have all graced its stage – alongside dazzling aerialists and jaw-dropping, partially unclothed dancers performing beneath high-tech LED screens.

The energy inside is unmatched, with deep bass thumping through the lavishly designed, neon-drenched space. Bottle service is the move here, but even if you're just soaking in the scene, it's impossible not to feel like you've entered a different dimension.

Pre-club, take the elevator up to **Giselle** (MAP: 17 P54 **B2**), the club's rooftop restaurant, where craft cocktails and luxe Asian-fusion bites set the tone, before diving into the madness below. And before you leave? Snag an E11EVEN Miami snapback hat, a legendary Miami nightlife souvenir that signals you've survived (and thrived in) the city's most infamous club.

Dine & Party in One at Komodo

RESTAURANT & NIGHTLIFE

MAP: 18 P54 **C8**

Few places capture Miami's club-staurant (yes, a restaurant meets club) energy like **Komodo** *(komodomiami.com)*, a David Grutman creation that blends high-energy nightlife with upscale Southeast Asian cuisine. Tucked in the heart of Brickell, this three-story hot spot sets the tone with sultry red lighting, lush jungle-inspired decor and a buzzing bar scene that often rivals the dining experience.

Grutman – also behind celeb-magnet spots such as Papi Steak, Casadonna and Gekko – knows how to curate a scene, and Komodo delivers with a DJ-driven soundtrack, an in-crowd sipping creative cocktails and a signature floating 'bird's nest' seating area that feels straight out of a Balinese dream. The menu is as bold as the ambience. Peking duck is the undisputed star, carved tableside to crispy, golden perfection. The truffle lo mein is a rich, umami-packed favorite, while the tuna and toro rolls and miso Chilean sea bass keep the sushi crowd happy. Dinner here isn't just a meal – it's an experience.

LISTINGS

Best Places for...

$ Budget $$ Midrange $$$ Top End

Eating

Chic

Quinto $$
 19 B7
Sexy rooftop with tropical greenery everywhere and incredible cocktails and fusion fare. *quintomiami.us, hours vary*

NIU Kitchen $$
20 B5
Stylish restaurant serving delectable, often shareable Catalan cuisine alongside a killer wine list. *niukitchen.com, 5:30-10pm Tue-Sun*

Verde $$
 21 C2
Inside the Pérez Art Museum Miami, this is a local favorite for its tasty market-fresh dishes and atmospheric setting. *pamm.org, 11am-4pm Fri-Mon, 11am-8pm Thu*

River Oyster Bar $$
22 B7
A few paces from the Miami River, this buzzing spot whips up excellent plates of seafood. *theriver miami.com, noon-10:30pm*

Around the World

Pollos & Jarras $$
23 C5
Peruvian spot serving up outstanding barbecued chicken (and chicken crackling – ie deep-fried skin – oh yes!). *pollosy jarras.squarespace.com, hours vary*

Bonding Thai $$
 24 B7
Multiple Asian cuisines, including Thai, Japanese and Korean, come together in a modern and trendy setting. *bonding thaimiami.com, hours vary*

Soya e Pomodoro $$
 25 B5
Feels like a bohemian Italian retreat, where you can dine on fresh pasta surrounded by vintage posters. *soyaepomodoro.com, hours vary*

CVI.CHE 105 $$
26 C5
Beautifully presented ceviches go down nicely with a round of specialty Peruvian cocktails. *ceviche105.squarespace.com, noon-10:30pm Sun-Thu, to 11:30 Fri & Sat*

Clubstraunts

Giselle $$$
see 17 B2
An opulent rooftop restaurant and lounge that blends French and Asian influences in a lavish, ultra-glam setting. *giselle miami.com, 6pm-1am Sun-Wed, to 3am Thu-Sat*

Sexy Fish $$$
 27 B8
A high-energy London import serving bold Japanese flavors in a surreal, art-filled space. *sexyfish miami.com, noon-midnight Sun-Wed, to 1am Thu-Sat*

Komodo $$$
see  18 C8
A high-end Southeast Asian hot spot with an indoor/outdoor vibe, signature Peking duck and a lively upstairs lounge for late-night fun. *komodomi ami.com, noon-midnight Sun-Wed, to 1am Thu-Sat*

Zuma $$$
 28 C6
This sleek, waterfront favorite delivers modern Japanese flavors with a buzzy yet sophisticated atmosphere. *zumarestau rant.com, noon-11pm Mon-Sat, 11:30am-11pm Sun*

Drinking

Hot Spots

Rosa Sky

29 A7

Rooftop cocktail bar in Brickell with jaw-dropping views of the Downtown Miami skyline. *rosaskyrooftop.com, 4:30pm-2am Tue-Sat, 2pm-1am Sun*

Blackbird Ordinary

30 A7

Late-night drinking spot with excellent cocktails that draw a neighborhood crowd. *blackbirdordinarymiami.com, 3pm-5am*

E11EVEN Miami

see 16 B2

Multilevel club and 'social playground' that promises an immersive experience. *11miami.com, hours vary*

Sugar

31 B8

Come for creative cocktails and Biscayne Bay views served on the tropical rooftop deck. *easthotels.com, hours vary*

Coffee Buzz

Puroast Coffee

see 24 B7

Low-acidity, high-flavor coffee brewed with a slow-roasting process for a smooth, rich cup. A cozy, no-fuss spot to grab a cup and linger. *puroast.com, 7am-6pm Mon-Fri, 8am-6pm Sat & Sun*

Pasion del Cielo

32 B8

A Brickell go-to for coffee purists, offering a variety of single-origin beans, roasted to perfection. *pasiondelcielocoffee.com, 7am-9pm Mon-Fri, 8am-9pm Sat & Sun*

Vibey Cocktail Bars

Baby Jane

33 B7

Part cocktail house part noodle bar, Baby Jane is a neon-lit Brickell mainstay where the good times roll. *babyjanemiami.com, noon-3am*

Mama Tried

34 B5

Moody 1970s-style bar with a speakeasy feel, giant metallic light fixtures and a retro-chic aesthetic. *4pm-5am Mon-Fri, 5pm-5am Sat & Sun*

Lost Boy

35 B5

Vintage Cuban furniture, exposed brick and old wood come together in this enormous pub. *lostboydrygoods.com, hours vary*

Black Market

36 B6

Quintessential sports bar with HD TVs on every conceivable surface, frosty beers and American pub grub. *blackmarketmia.com, hours vary*

Shopping

Shopping Centers

Brickell City Centre

37 B7

A sleek, open-air retail paradise featuring high-end fashion, trendy boutiques and an upscale food hall. *brickellcitycentre.com, 10am-9:30pm Mon-Sat, noon-7pm Sun*

Bayside Marketplace

see Bayside Marketplace C4

A waterfront shopping and entertainment hub packed with souvenir shops, casual eateries and live music, all with stunning views of Biscayne Bay. *baysidemarketplace.com, 10am-10pm Mon-Sat, 11am-9pm Sun*

Mary Brickell Village

38 B8

A charming mix of local boutiques, stylish shops and lively restaurants, perfect for a laid-back stroll or a weekend brunch outing. *marybrickellvillage.com, 10am-9pm Mon-Sat, noon-6pm Sun*

See p85 for eating, drinking and shopping listings

Explore Wynwood & the Design District

Wynwood and the Design District are where Miami's creative energy and high-end design collide. Once a hub of warehouses and factories, Wynwood transformed in the early 2000s as artists and entrepreneurs reimagined its industrial spaces, turning them into bold street art galleries, hip breweries and experimental eateries. Just north, the Design District evolved from a forgotten showroom district into a luxury shopping and culinary haven. Today, these neighboring enclaves are a striking contrast – Wynwood is raw and artistic, the Design District sleek and curated – yet together, they showcase Miami's ever-evolving style that's sought the world over.

Getting Around

Buses & Trolleys

The Metrobus and Miami Trolley make reaching Wynwood from Downtown Miami easy. You can hop on the Metrobus Route 2 or the Biscayne-Brickell Trolley for a free ride to the area.

Walk

By day, it's a manageable 1-mile walk between Wynwood and the Design District. The route is not the most scenic, but it's straightforward.

Car & Rideshare

Street parking is plentiful but metered. At night, a taxi or rideshare is the safest and easiest way to get between these districts or beyond.

THE BEST

GRAFFITI ART Wynwood Walls (p76)

CONTEMPORARY ART Margulies Collection at the Warehouse (p82)

HIP MARKETPLACE Wynwood Marketplace (p80)

FOODIE HAVEN Smorgasburg Miami (p81)

Mural artist Ktano, Wynwood
FELIX MIZIOZNIKOV/SHUTTERSTOCK

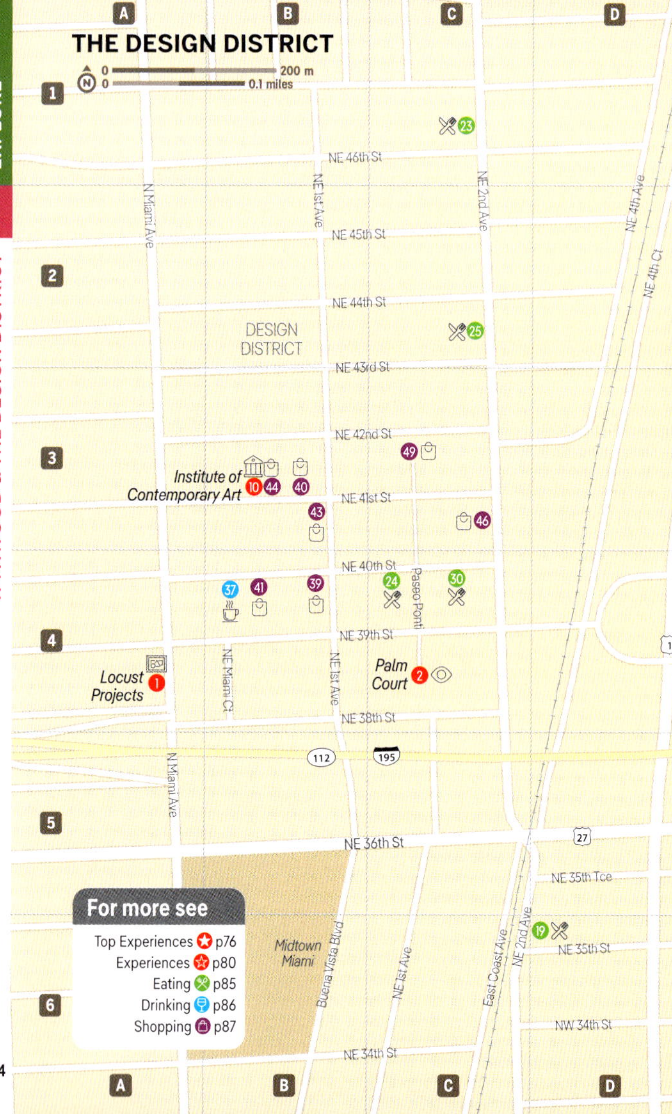
THE DESIGN DISTRICT
0 200 m
0 0.1 miles
A
B
C
D
1
2
3
4
5
6
NE 46th St
NE 45th St
NE 44th St
NE 43rd St
NE 42nd St
NE 41st St
NE 40th St
NE 39th St
NE 38th St
NE 36th St
NE 35th Tce
NE 35th St
NW 34th St
NE 34th St
N Miami Ave
NE 1st Ave
NE 2nd Ave
NE 4th Ave
NE 4th Ct
NE Miami Ct
Paseo Ponti
Buena Vista Blvd
East Coast Ave
DESIGN DISTRICT
Institute of Contemporary Art
Locust Projects
Palm Court
Midtown Miami
112
195
27
1
23
25
49
10
44
40
43
46
37
41
39
24
30
2
19
For more see
Top Experiences p76
Experiences p80
Eating p85
Drinking p86
Shopping p87

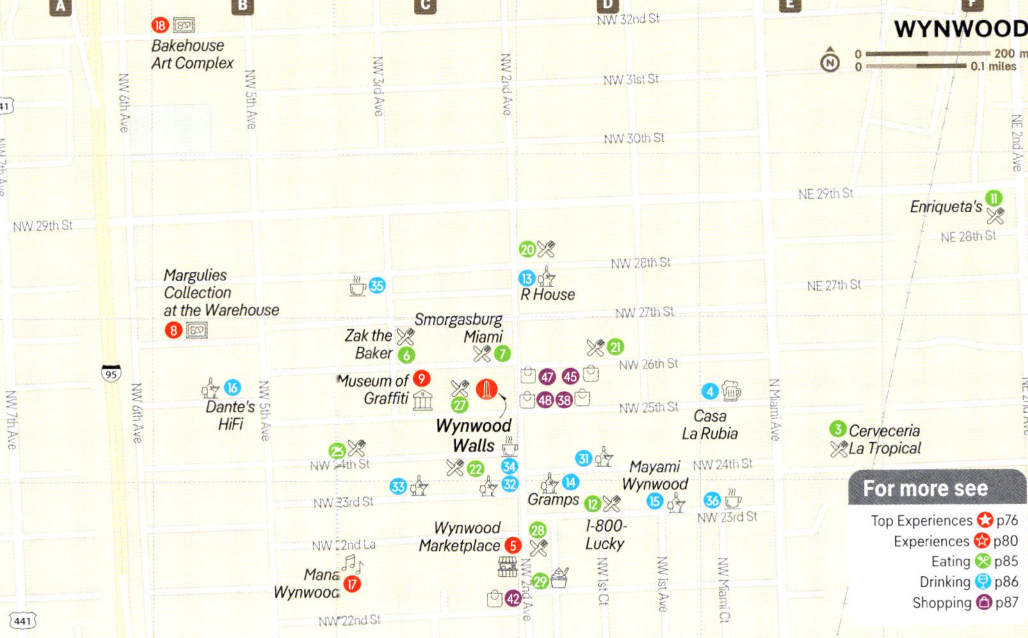
WYNWOOD
0 200 m
0 0.1 miles
A
B
C
D
E
F
1
2
3
4
Bakehouse Art Complex
Margulies Collection at the Warehouse
Dante's HiFi
Zak the Baker
Smorgasburg Miami
Museum of Graffiti
Wynwood Walls
R House
Gramps
Mayami Wynwood
1-800-Lucky
Wynwood Marketplace
Mana Wynwood
Casa La Rubia
Cerveceria La Tropical
Enriqueta's
NW 32nd St
NW 31st St
NW 30th St
NW 29th St
NE 29th St
NW 28th St
NE 28th St
NW 27th St
NE 27th St
NW 26th St
NW 25th St
NW 24th St
NW 23rd St
NW 22nd St
NW 7th Ave
NW 6th Ave
NW 5th Ave
NW 3rd Ave
NW 2nd Ave
NW 1st Ct
NW 1st Ave
NW Miami Ct
N Miami Ave
NE 2nd Ave
441
95
For more see
Top Experiences p76
Experiences p80
Eating p85
Drinking p86
Shopping p87

★ TOP EXPERIENCE

Wynwood Walls

The launch of Wynwood Walls created waves in the contemporary-art world that ripple to this day. It came in the form of eye-popping, color-saturated murals blanketing the walls of a former warehouse district. Artists from around the world have added their touch to this ever-changing open-air gallery, transforming Wynwood into an epicenter for public art.

MAP P75 **C3**

PLANNING TIP
The space is open from 10:30am to 6:30pm daily. As a large part of the art spaces are outside, time your visit early in the morning or in the later afternoon to avoid the South Florida heat.

Scan this QR code to peruse the various themed tours on-site.

A Canvas Transformed

In 2009 developer Tony Goldman saw potential in Wynwood's drab warehouse exteriors. He invited renowned street artists to reimagine these blank canvases, creating what is now one of the most famous outdoor street art museums in the world: the **Wynwood Walls** *(wynwoodwalls.com; adult/child $12/free)*. The project started with six warehouse buildings, their solid, windowless facades providing the backdrop for large-scale murals. From the start, the Walls featured an impressive lineup of international street art legends, including Shepard Fairey (of *Obey* and *Hope* fame), Brazil's Os Gemeos and Invader from France. Today more than 100 artists from 21 countries have left their mark, including Japan's Aiko and Portugal's Alexandre Farto (aka Vhils), who 'carves' instead of paints, sometimes using a jackhammer to etch hyper-realistic portraits into concrete.

One of the most extraordinary aspects of Wynwood Walls is its ephemeral nature. The average lifespan of a mural here is less than a year before it's painted over by another artist. No two visits look quite the same, mirroring the ever-evolving essence of street art itself.

MATTHEWS MARKS GALLERY/COURTESY OF ART BASEL

Art Basel & Beyond

What began as an ambitious experiment gained international acclaim when **Art Basel Miami Beach** *(artbasel.com)*, an international art show (pictured) with a Miami engagement in December, came to town. Thousands of art lovers and collectors descended on Wynwood to admire the striking, large-scale murals. The Walls became a cultural magnet, helping spur Wynwood's transformation from a sleepy warehouse district into one of Miami's most vibrant neighborhoods. Though the art changes, themes remain bold. Many murals tackle homelessness, police brutality, materialism and social inequality, while others embrace science-fiction dreamscapes or portraits of icons like Martin Luther King Jr, Bob Marley and – sure – Yoda.

QUICK BREAK

Pop Into **Panther Coffee** (p86) – the neighborhood's original coffeehouse and a Miami-wide favorite – for a pour-over coffee or latte-art pizzazz-ed beverage. Chill on its patio for prime people-watching.

WALKING TOUR

Walk the Design District

The Miami Design District is a visible shift from neighboring Wynwood's edginess. Here, you'll find the most lux of global shops, intertwined with public art displays, murals and upscale eateries with crowds that often like to linger. It's all a very strollable and condensed experience (roughly a two-by-five-block square), primed for families and couples alike.

START	END	LENGTH
Institute for Contemporary Art	City View Garage	0.6mi; 3 hours

1 Cutting-Edge Canvas

Start your exploration of the Design District with bold exhibitions showcasing avant-garde works by emerging and established artists at the **Institute of Contemporary Art**. Explore rotating galleries, an outdoor sculpture garden and interactive installations – all free of charge. Expect a mix of experimental art, immersive exhibits and dynamic cultural programming. A free guided tour is given daily.

2 A Paradise Pop

Wander over to **Paradise Plaza** for two of the district's architectural marvels. The Johnston Marklee & Associates Façade draws the eye to the Miami sky with its features that accentuate the neighborhood's existing urban fabric. Tolila + Gilliland used terra-cotta tiles inspired by the colors of Miami's natural environment in patterns influenced by Miami's rich history.

3 Urban Arches

Picture-perfect **Jade Alley** is the ultimate backdrop, with pieces like Daniel Toole's *Arches*, tall concrete arches implicative of Roman aqueducts meant to inspire wonder and intimacy. They were cast in wooden molds that left a natural imprint resulting in an organic installation. Jade Alley also houses works by Urs Fischer, Amani Lewis and Virgil Abloh.

4 Above Water Aquatics

Become one with the art along **Paseo Ponti**. Feel like a kid again on *Conscious Actions*, gt2P's colorful swing set. Climb onto the *Support System*, geodome monkey bar play structures designed by Dozie Kanu. Take a break beneath blue and green hues of sculptural shade structures containing fish and aquatic vegetation created by brothers Ronan & Erwan Bouroullec.

5 It's Like a Jungle

It might seem like you're walking onto the set of a sci-fi film, but it's really the innovative pieces by Buckminster Fuller, Xavier Veilhan and Sou Fujimoto taking center stage in **Palm Court** (p80). *Fly's Eye Dome* is a large airy dome that mimics, you guessed it, a fly's eye. Also in the courtyard is a giant geometric-esque bust (Le Corbusier) that appears to be growing from the ground beneath a shimmering glass and steel facade that gives the illusion of a waterfall.

6 Car Park Pop

City View Garage isn't just for parking: it's a bold architectural statement. Designed by artists and architects, its vibrant facades feature geometric blue aluminum panels by Leong Leong and a striking metal mesh design by IwamotoScott. This fusion of function and art makes it a true Design District landmark.

EXPERIENCES

Dabble in the Design District

ART & ARCHITECTURE

Even the Design District's parking garages lean into the design aesthetic, making every corner of this neighborhood a curated visual experience. A focal point is **Locust Projects** (MAP: 1 P74 **A4**; *locustprojects.org; free*), Miami's longest-running nonprofit experimental art space. Since 1998 it has featured work from 250-plus artists, focusing on site-specific installations that push creative limits. Unlike commercial galleries, Locust Projects prioritizes process-driven work and sometimes wacky ideas, often showcasing projects that wouldn't fit into more traditional art venues. Nearby, **Palm Court** (MAP: 2 P74 **C4**) serves as both a pedestrian plaza and a display space for large-scale public art, especially come Art Basel time. The area is anchored by Buckminster Fuller's *Fly's Eye Dome,* a 24ft geodesic sphere originally designed in the 1960s. Surrounding the plaza, high-end retailers sit alongside contemporary sculptures, making this a central spot for design enthusiasts to take in Miami's landscape. It's worth a peruse or sit down to take it all in.

Sip on Some Cervezas

BEER & BREWERIES

Sure, Wynwood is best known for its murals, but its craft beer scene has steadily grown alongside the art. Among the breweries drawing locals and visitors alike, **Cerveceria La Tropical** (MAP: 3 P75 **E3**; *cervercerialatropical.com*) stands out for its deep Cuban roots. Originally founded in Havana in 1888, the brand was revived in Miami, where its tropical-garden-style beer hall has house-brewed lagers, live music and a menu featuring Caribbean-influenced bites. The brewery combines a sports bar atmosphere with an outdoor space filled with lush greenery. A few blocks away, **Casa La Rubia** (MAP: 4 P75 **E3**; *larubia.beer*) – formerly Veza Sur – operates as a boutique brewery with a more understated approach. Its focus is now on small-batch, European-style lagers, offering an alternative to the heavier IPAs that dominate a growing number of South Florida breweries.

Explore Wynwood Marketplace's Eclectic Attractions

SHOPPING & SOCIAL SPACES

MAP: 5 P75 **C4**

The **Wynwood Marketplace** (*wynwoodmarketplace.com*) blends food stalls, pop-up shops, live entertainment and unexpected social activities into a sprawling, open-air venue. It's equal parts night market, beer garden and event space, shifting in energy depending on the time of day and year. For an unusual activity, check out **Sip & Pickle** (*sipandpickle.com; per hour from $58*), a bar-side pickleball court where you can play a casual match while sipping a drink. The atmosphere leans social rather than competitive, making it an approachable option even for first-timers. Its shipping container surrounds make for a nice artsy selfie, too. Beyond pickleball, the marketplace features rotating vendors selling everything from handmade jewelry to Latin street food. The main bar area is a focal point in the evenings, with DJ sets and themed nights drawing a mix of locals and tourists.

Fuel Your Morning at Zak the Baker

BAKERY & CAFE

MAP: 6 P75 C3

Right up there on Miami's most beloved bakery list, **Zak the Baker** *(zakthebaker.com)* has become a neighborhood fixture, drawing steady crowds for its simple but well-executed bread, pastries and deli-style meals. The bakery's focus is on naturally fermented sourdough, with a menu that shifts based on seasonal ingredients and kosher dietary guidelines. The counter-service setup moves quickly, with lines often forming out the door, especially during weekend mornings. The bread selection is the main draw, with varieties like country sourdough, seeded rye and challah available daily. For those staying to eat, options range from smoked fish plates and *shakshuka* to sandwiches built on thick slices of house-made bread. No skimping on portions here. Beyond buying some bread on-site to take home, you can also snag select Zak the Baker offerings at select Whole Foods grocery stores *(wholefoodmarkets.com)* throughout the Miami area. It's a further testament to just how beloved ole Zak has become.

Taste It All at Smorgasburg Miami

FOOD MARKET

MAP: 7 P75 C3

Smorgasburg Miami *(smorgas burgmiami.com)* is an outdoor food market with a rotating lineup of vendors selling everything from

BACARDI IN MIAMI

The former Miami headquarters of Bacardi, located at 2100 Biscayne Blvd, is a masterpiece of tropical architecture and holds a spot on the National Register of Historic Places. The main event is a beautifully decorated, jewel-box-like building built in 1973 that seems to hover over the ground, supported by a central pillar. One-inch-thick pieces of hammered glass cover the exterior in a wild Mesoamerican-style pattern modeled after a mosaic designed by German artist Johannes M Dietz. Also on-site is the older 1963 building, a tower covered with blue-and-white handmade tiles – some 28,000, in fact – in a striking ceramic pattern designed by Brazilian artist Francisco Brennand.

BEST NEIGHBORHOOD MUSEUMS

Margulies Collection at the Warehouse

MAP: 8 P75 B3

A renowned contemporary art space featuring photography, sculpture and video installations in a massive, repurposed warehouse.

Museum of Graffiti

MAP: 9 P75 C3

The world's first museum dedicated to graffiti, showcasing street art's evolution through exhibits, murals and artist retrospectives.

Institute of Contemporary Art

MAP: 10 P74 B3

Offers free admission and bold exhibitions, with emerging and established artists in a totally sleek space.

loaded tacos to gourmet desserts. Originally launched in Brooklyn, the Miami iteration follows a similar model, offering a changing selection of small, independent food businesses. The vendors vary from week to week, but staples dabble in street offerings, plant-based dishes and experimental desserts. So, Korean corn dogs, Argentine empanadas and Japanese soufflé pancakes – they're all fair game and often primed for an Instagram photo (or 10). The market's setup is informal – seating is scattered and most people eat standing or perched on shared benches. It's all in a gravel parking lot, adding that much more to the charm. Expect long lines at popular vendors, especially during weekend hours. Pack your sunscreen, too, as it gets hot eating in the beating sun.

Step into Old Miami at Enriqueta's

LOCAL EATS

MAP: 11 P75 F2

Before Wynwood became an international arts hub, locals gathered at **Enriqueta's** *(facebook.com/enriquetassandwichshop)* – and they still do. This unassuming Cuban diner remains one of the last holdouts of old Miami in the 'hood, serving up strong coffee, hearty sandwiches and a dose of nostalgia that's equally as appetizing. Spanish conversations buzz over plates of *pan con bistec* (steak sandwiches), crispy *croquetas* and classic Cuban sandwiches. Daily specials like *lechón asado* (roast pork) and *picadillo* (spiced ground beef) keep the regulars coming back, too.

Save an Appetite for 1-800-Lucky

FOOD & NIGHTLIFE

MAP: 12 P75 D4

This lively Asian food hall fuses culture, cuisine and nightlife under one roof, creating an experience as transportive as it is delicious. Step inside (or outside, as there is a bustling patio area) and you're immediately immersed in a sensory overload: red lanterns glow

Zak the Baker (p81)

overhead, hip-hop pulses through the speakers and stylish diners sip cocktails at the sleek bar. The food? A mix of damn-good Asian street eats, from pork belly bao and sashimi bowls to Thai-style chicken wings. As the night progresses, **1-800-Lucky** *(1800lucky.com)* morphs into a bustling outdoor party, where craft cocktails flow as freely as the conversation. Pro-tips: book the private karaoke room on-site if you're feeling vocal and don't end the night without some matcha ice cream from the stall outside.

Take a Hike Through Wynwood

TOURS

One of the best ways to take in the Miami art scene is to join in the **Wynwood Art Walk Block Party**, held on the second Saturday of every month. Many galleries around Wynwood host special events and art openings, with ever-flowing drinks (not always free), live music, food trucks and special markets.

Another way to see the neighborhood is the similarly named **Wynwood Art Walk** *(wynwoodartwalk.com)*. This 'walk' is actually a 90-minute guided tour to some of the best gallery shows of the day, plus a look at some interesting street art around the 'hood. It also offers other tours like a golf-cart trip around the area's best graffiti.

Drag Yourself into R House

FOOD & NIGHTLIFE

MAP: 13 P75 D2

R House *(rhousewynwood.com)* hosts some of the best drag performances in all of Miami. Brunch is the star of the show – every Saturday and Sunday, its legendary

BEST NEIGHBORHOOD MUSIC VENUES

Gramps

MAP: 14 P75 **D4**

A beloved bar and venue hosting live music, comedy and DJs, with a retro vibe, craft cocktails and a spacious outdoor patio.

Mayami Wynwood

MAP: 15 P75 **D4**

A lively spot blending Latin beats, DJs and live performances with a wild open-air design.

Dante's HiFi

MAP: 16 P75 **B3**

Miami's first vinyl listening bar, with an intimate, high-fidelity sound experience and curated DJ sets in an uber-cozy space.

Mana Wynwood

MAP: 17 P75 **C4**

A massive event venue hosting concerts, festivals and large-scale music experiences, like the increasingly popular III Points festival.

Drag Brunch brings endless mimosas, towering plates of chicken and waffles, and truly jaw-dropping performances from top drag queens from near and far. Expect high-energy routines, lip-sync battles and an all-around party vibe that has made it a local fav. On Fridays R House often transforms into an electrifying dinner party, featuring live DJs and performers. Midweek visitors can enjoy a more laid-back experience, where the restaurant's colorful murals and stylish indoor-outdoor setup shine.

Pro-tips: book your brunch table in advance – it sells out fast. For the best views, request a seat near the main stage. And if you're feeling bold, don't be surprised if you're pulled into the show. Get ready, you've been warned.

Get Creative at Bakehouse Art Complex

ARTS & CULTURE

MAP: 18 P75 **B1**

Tucked away in a former art deco-era bakery, **Bakehouse Art Complex** *(bacfl.org)* is one of Miami's best-kept secrets for contemporary art lovers. This dynamic artist hub is home to over 100 resident artists, offering visitors an inside look at Miami's thriving creative community. Unlike traditional galleries, Bakehouse is a working studio space where guests can watch artists at work, explore rotating exhibitions and even chat with creatives about their process.

For hands-on experiences, Bakehouse offers art workshops ranging from ceramics and printmaking to figure drawing. These classes are open to the public and cater to both beginners and seasoned artists looking to refine their craft.

On the first Friday of every month, Open Studio Nights invites guests to wander through the artist studios, enjoy live demonstrations and discover one-of-a-kind pieces available for purchase.

Best Places for...

$ Budget $$ Midrange $$$ Top End

Eating

International

La Latina $

19 p74 **D6**

Popular with both Midtown locals and transplants who dig into arepas, pulled pork and Venezuelan favorites. *lalatinamiami.com, 9am-10pm Sun-Thu, to 4pm Fri & Sat*

Bakan $$

20 p75 **D2**

Live the good ceviche and *aguachile* (marinated shrimp) life at this lively Mexican restaurant with a fab mezcal selection. *bakanwynwood.com, noon-11pm Sun-Wed, to 2am Thu-Sat*

Piegari $$$

21 p75 **D3**

Upscale Italian (via Argentina) spot near Wynwood known for freshly made pastas like squid ink fettuccine with shrimp. *piegariristorante.com, 12:30pm-11pm Sun-Thu, to 11:30pm Fri & Sat*

Rishtedar $$

22 p75 **C3**

Communal Indian favorite with a colorful exterior and equally as colorful traditional and innovative dishes. Enjoy the flower-inspired ceiling, too. *rishtedar.com, noon-10pm Sun-Thu, to 11pm Fri & Sat*

Cheap Eats

Enriqueta's $

see 11 p75 **F2**

No-frills Cuban diner with daily specials and great Cuban sandwiches and coffee. *7am-3pm Mon-Fri, to 2pm Sat*

1-800-Lucky $

see 12 p75 **D4**

Miami's take on an Asian hawker market, with tons of street food and Wynwood neon to boot. *1800lucky.com, noon-1am Mon-Thu, to 3am Fri-Sun*

Lemoni Café $

23 p74 **C1**

European cafe vibes serving delicious French toast, paninis and pancakes with plenty of outdoor seating. *lemoni-cafe.com, 10am-8pm*

Splurge-Worthy

Michael's Genuine $$$

24 p74 **C4**

A tavern-turned-temple to New American cuisine, serving up locally sourced comfort food and buzzing crowds. *michaelsgenuine.com, 11:30am-11pm Mon-Sat, 11am-10pm Sun*

Mandolin Aegean Bistro $$$

25 p74 **C2**

It's all Mediterranean whites and blues at this Design District gem, serving grilled bass, lamb, kebabs and more. *mandolinrestaurant.com, noon-11pm*

Doya $$$

26 p75 **C3**

Meze plates from Greece and Turkey are ideal for sharing at this lively Wynwood Aegean-inspired restaurant. *doyarestaurant.com, noon-midnight*

Kyu $$$

27 p75 **C3**

Go all in on umami at this sublime Wynwood Asian restaurant that has mastered the art of Japanese wood-fired grilling. *kyurestaurants.com, 5pm-10pm Mon & Tue, noon-10pm Wed-Sun*

Bakeries & Treats

Yann Couvreur Café $$

28 p75 **D4**

Miami outpost of a Parisian chef in the geographic heart of Wynwood, with classic French pastries that make the heart flutter. *cafe.yanncouvreur.us, 8am-6pm Mon-Fri, 9am-7pm Sat & Sun*

Dasher & Crank $

29 p75 **D4**

Quite literally churns out ice cream, ranging from passion fruit sorbet to (of course) mojito. *dasherandcrank.com, noon-11pm*

Zak the Baker $

see 6 p75 **C3**

An artisan kosher bakery helmed by a Miami native; known for ridiculously good pastries and BLTs on croissants. *zakthebaker.com, 7am-5pm Sun-Fri*

Tablé by Antonio Bachour $

30 p74 **C4**

A chic Parisian-style brasserie with Miami and Lebanese influences, serving up world-class pastries and plenty more. *tablebachour.com, 8am-7pm Mon-Sat, to 5pm Sun*

Drinking

Cocktail Bars

Dirty Rabbit

31 p75 **D3**

Colorful cocktails, edgy-but-cute art and live music attract the cool kids. *the-dirtyrabbit.com, hours vary*

Dante's HiFi

see 16 p75 B3

Have an excellent cocktail in a laid-back lounge that doubles as a vinyl listening room. *danteshifi.com, hours vary*

Coyo Taco

32 p75 **C4**

There's a secret bar hidden behind a killer taco stand here, where DJs draw the crowds. *coyo-taco.com, hours vary*

Drinks & Entertainment

Gramps

see 14 p75 **D4**

Everyone loves this super laid-back spot for its cold beer, strong cocktails, live DJs,and Thursday drag shows. *gramps.com, noon-1am Sun-Thu, to 3am Fri & Sat*

R House

see 13 p75 **D2**

A favorite for weekend drag brunches served up with revelry, bottomless white-wine sangrias and mojitos. *rhousewynwood.com, hours vary*

Selvatico

33 p75 **C4**

A jungle-inspired bar near Wynwood Walls that feels like you've snuck into a secret forest to sip herbaceous mojitos. *selvaticowynwood.com, 7pm-3am Thu-Sat*

Coffee

Panther Coffee

34 p75 **C3**

A Miami classic for small-batch roasted coffee and industrial-chic vibes. *panthercoffee.com, 7am-6pm*

Miam Cafe

35 p75 **C2**

Cozy spot serving great coffee and light bites in a laid-back Wynwood space. *miamcafe.com, 8am-5pm*

Salty Donut

36 p75 **E4**

Artisan doughnut shop offering a variety of intricate, massive craft doughnuts paired with quality coffee. *saltydonut.com, 7am-7pm Mon-Fri, 8am-7pm Sat & Sun*

BIGFACE

37 p74 **B4**

Ex-Miami Heat star Jimmy Butler's venture into specialty coffee, with an espresso bar, grab-and-go options and exclusive merch. *bigfacebrand.com, 9am-6pm Mon-Sat, to 5pm Sun*

Shopping

Men's & Women's Fashion

OFY

38 p75 **D3**

Men's and women's clothing store near Wynwood Walls with stylish loungewear and fun Florida-themed collections. *ofyshop.com, 11am-8pm Mon-Sat, noon-6pm Sun*

Alice + Olivia

39 p74 **B4**

Women's clothing boutique known for designer denim and beautiful print dresses. *aliceandolivia.com, 11am-8pm*

Acne Studios

40 p74 **B3**

Italian leather and Japanese denim are among the elite raw ingredients in this cult Swedish atelier's stable. *acnestudios.com, 11am-8pm Mon-Sat, noon-6pm Sun*

GANNI

41 p74 B4

If it's cool enough for Copenhagen's cool girls, you'll find the Scandinavian fashion favorite here. *ganni.com, 11am-7pm Mon-Sat, noon-6pm Sun*

Sneakers & Streetwear

Sole Garden

42 p75 **C4**

Upscale sneaker consignment shop with some of the coolest kicks around (you can get yours freshened up here, too). *thesolegarden.com, noon-8pm Mon-Sat, to 7pm Sun*

Golden Goose

43 p74 **B3**

There are sneakers, and then there's this beloved high-fashion Italian brand known for its emblematic star. *goldengoose.com, 11am-8pm Mon-Sat, noon-6pm Sun*

KITH

44 p74 **B3**

A sleek concept store blending high-end streetwear, sneakers and lifestyle goods. Expect limited-edition drops, exclusive collaborations and a stylish crowd. *kith.com, 11am-8pm Mon-Sat, noon-6pm Sun*

Perfumes & Beauty

Osme

45 p75 **D3**

Unique perfumery and apothecary catering to those obsessed with natural scents and olfactory delights. *osmeperfumery.com, 11am-7pm Mon-Sat, noon-6pm Sun*

Maison Francis Kurkdjian

46 p74 **C3**

Pop in for a signature scent from this luxury French perfumery. *franciskurkdjian.com, 11am-8pm Mon-Sat, noon-6pm Sun*

Swimwear & Accessories

Capelle

47 p75 **D3**

Who couldn't use designer swim trunks from this cheerful and rainbow-colored flagship store of the Miami-based brand? *capellemiami.com, 11am-7pm Mon-Sat, noon-6pm Sun*

The Wynwood Shop

48 p75 **D3**

Sunglasses, resort-inspired jewelry and stylish pickleball bags are among the accessories to help you live your best 305 (fun fact, Miami's area code) life. *wynwoodshop.com, 11am-8pm Mon-Sat, noon-6pm Sun*

Isa Grutman

49 p74 **C3**

Intimate collection of elegant and timeless selections, all crafted with natural diamonds and gemstones. *isagrutman.com, 11am-8pm*

★ WORTH A TRIP

Rubell Museum

A must-visit for contemporary art lovers, the Rubell Museum *(rubellmuseum.org; adult/youth $15/10)* delivers a powerhouse lineup of cutting-edge works in a sprawling, industrial-chic space. Thoughtfully curated exhibitions showcase bold, provocative pieces from art-world heavyweights, making this a top spot to experience Miami's thriving creative pulse and one of the city's most burgeoning neighborhoods, Allapattah.

GETTING THERE
The Rubell Museum is tucked on the west side of Interstate 95 in the Allapattah neighborhood, which is due west of Wynwood. It's a five-minute rideshare trip from Wynwood.

Scan this QR code to see the museum's latest exhibition roster.

Evolution of a Powerhouse Collection

Don and Mera Rubell began collecting art in 1964 and over the decades their sharp instincts for spotting the Next Big Thing have shaped one of the most significant contemporary art collections in the world. Originally housed in Wynwood, since relocating to Allapattah in 2019 the museum has played a pivotal role in the neighborhood's transformation from gritty warehouse district to international art hub. The Allapattah space is a sprawling 53,000-square-foot complex of six former industrial buildings, reimagined by Selldorf Architects into one of the largest private contemporary art institutions in North America.

Forty Galleries of Brilliance

Walking through the Rubell Museum is like a crash course in contemporary art's greatest hits. With 40 galleries filled with work by heavyweights like Kehinde Wiley, Jeff Koons, Cindy Sherman and Cady Noland, the collection doesn't just highlight major names, it cements their influence. Unlike many institutions that rely on rotating exhibits, the Rubell keeps a strong foundation, with roughly 65% of its space dedicated to long-term holdings and 35% reserved for special exhibitions.

ZUMA PRESS/ALAMY STOCK PHOTO

This means returning visitors can always expect a balance of the familiar and the fresh.

Curating with an Edge

The museum is known for its razor-sharp thematic exhibitions, often tackling urgent social and political issues. In *30 Americans*, one of its most celebrated traveling shows, the museum showcased works from prominent Black artists like Kara Walker, Hank Willis Thomas and Mickalene Thomas, confronting race, identity and history in America. Another standout, *NO MAN'S LAND*, put women artists at the forefront, featuring works from Cindy Sherman, Cecily Brown and Jenny Holzer. The Rubell doesn't just collect, it builds careers. Artists like Keith Haring and Jean-Michel Basquiat were acquired early, long before they became household names.

QUICK BREAK
Within a 15-minute stroll southeast, you'll arrive at the **World Famous House of Mac**, which bedazzles mac and cheese with jerk chicken, smoked barbecue and more creative ingredients.

★ WORTH A TRIP

Superblue Miami

Superblue Miami *(superblue.com; adult/child $32/17)* is a full-sensory experience. This edgy space has larger-than-life installations that move and respond. With a lineup of high-tech visionaries like teamLab, Es Devlin and James Turrell, this is where Miami's art scene enters a new dimension.

GETTING THERE
Superblue is across the street from Rubell Museum (p88) – for making the most of an Allapattah rideshare, you'll want to pair the two experiences together.

An Art Movement Lands in Miami

Superblue's arrival in 2021 marked a turning point for Miami's art scene, positioning the city within a global movement of immersive art experiences. While Miami is known for its street murals and traditional galleries, Superblue offers something completely different: an interactive playground where technology, nature and human perception have a party together.

Superblue joins the ranks of similar experiential museums – think teamLab Borderless in Tokyo, L'Atelier des Lumières in Paris and ARTECHOUSE in Washington, DC (and in Miami Beach, too), all of which explore the intersection of art and digital innovation. Unlike traditional museums, Superblue has rotating large-scale installations designed to evolve over time, ensuring there's always something new to discover.

Step Inside the Art

Superblue Miami takes immersive art to the next level, offering exhibits that don't just hang on walls – they really kind of envelop you. One of its standout installations is *Massless Clouds Between Sculpture and Life* by teamLab, where visitors walk through floating clouds of bubbles that dissolve on contact. The experience is mesmerizing and unpredictable, making each step through the space completely unique. Another jaw-dropping

Scan this QR code for current exhibitions and ticket info.

FOREST OF US BY ES DELVIN/COURTESY OF SUPERBLUE

piece is *Forest of Us* by Es Devlin (pictured), a mirrored labyrinth that plays with light and reflection, creating a disorienting but beautiful visual experience inspired by the structure of human lungs.

Your Heartbeat, but Make It Art

Superblue doesn't just make you look – it makes you feel. Rafael Lozano-Hemmer's *Pulse Topology* installation turns visitors into living artworks, using biometric sensors to capture individual heartbeats and translate them into pulsating lights across 3000 suspended bulbs. Walk through the space, and you'll literally see the rhythm of life glowing all around you. Meanwhile, James Turrell's *AKHU* immerses you in shifting hues of pure light, creating an almost meditative atmosphere that plays tricks on your perception.

QUICK BREAK

A 180° turn from all the sensory overload, **Morgans Restaurant**, a 15-minute stroll from Superblue, has classic American fare in an old house-gone-restaurant.

See p101
for eating,
drinking and
shopping
listings

Explore
Little Havana

Little Havana's Cuba-ness may be exaggerated for visitors, but it remains atmospheric, with domino clacks, cigar smoke and salsa beats ever-radiating. Murals range from Cuban Revolution tributes to modern hip-hop and *Miami Heat* references. The heart of the neighborhood, Calle Ocho, is liveliest on weekends, where old-timers banter over dominoes in Máximo Gómez Park and galleries showcase contemporary art. Shop for souvenirs and cigars, sip strong coffee and return for Cuban fare before catching live music at a salsa club. The best-known Cuban American neighborhood in the US, Little Havana was declared a national treasure by the National Trust for Historic Preservation in 2017.

Getting Around

Walking

Exploring Little Havana on foot is the best way to soak in its atmosphere. Most attractions along Calle Ocho are within a manageable stroll, and being on the street – among Cubans, Cuban Americans and visitors alike – is part of the experience.

Buses

The number 8 bus from Brickell Station runs every 10 to 20 minutes, making the 15-minute journey to Little Havana an easy and affordable option.

Bicycles

A Citi Bike station at SW 8th St and 10th Ave offers a convenient way to explore on two wheels.

THE BEST

LIVE PERFORMANCES Cubaocho (p98)

DOMINO GAMES Máximo Gómez Park (p100)

ARTSY STROLL Little Havana Art District (p98)

CUBAN-INSPIRED COCKTAILS Café La Trova (p98)

SALSA LESSONS Ball & Chain (p98)

Domino player in Máximo Gómez Park (p100)
FOTOLUMINATE LLC/SHUTTERSTOCK

For more see

Top Experiences p95
Experiences p98
Eating p101
Drinking p101
Shopping p101

0 500 m
0 0.25 miles

A B C D E F
1 2 3 4

Cuban Memorial Boulevard Park
Café La Trova
Los Pinareños Frutería
Cubaocho
Azucar Ice Cream
Ball & Chain
Lung Yai Thai Tapas
Máximo Gómez Park
Viernes Culturales
LITTLE HAVANA
CORAL WAY

W Flagler St
SW 1st St
SW 2nd St
SW 3rd St
SW 4th St
SW 5th St
SW 6th St
SW 7th St
SW 8th St (Calle Ocho)
SW 9th St
SW 10th St
SW 11th St
SW 21st Ave
SW 20th Ave
SW 19th Ave
SW 18th Ct
SW 18th Ave
SW 17th Ct
SW 17th Ave
SW 16th Ave
SW 15th Ave
SW 14th Ave
SW 13th Ct
SW 13th Ave
Cuban Memorial Blvd
SW 12th Ct
SW 12th Ave
SW 11th Ave

★ TOP EXPERIENCE

Cuban Memorial Boulevard Park

Cuban Memorial Boulevard Park is a testament to an island that thousands of Miamians have never set foot on, yet remains integral to their identity. It's a skinny space occupying the median of SW 13th Ave. There are scattered memorials, taking some cultural context to appreciate.

A Tribute to Cuban Exiles

Cuban Memorial Boulevard Park is a reflective space where Cuban American families and visitors pause to honor the past. The park's most striking feature is the Eternal Torch of Brigade 2506, dedicated to the soldiers who lost their lives during the failed 1961 Bay of Pigs invasion. Nearby, a bronze statue of Néstor 'Tony' Izquierdo, a veteran of the invasion who later fought against communism in Nicaragua, further emphasizes the park's anti-communist theme.

PLANNING TIP

The park is effectively always open, but is best visited in the early morning or around sunset; the heat of the day is less baking and there is sometimes an air of quiet (for Miami) reverence.

Monuments of Cuban History

The park is rich with other symbolic tributes to Cuban heritage and resistance. A statue of the Virgin Mary offers a spiritual presence, while a bust of Antonio Maceo Grajales, a hero of the Cuban War of Independence, connects visitors to Cuba's long struggle for freedom. A bronze map of Cuba stands as a nostalgic reminder of the homeland, and the Plaza de los Periodistas Cubanos honors exiled Cuban journalists who challenged the Castro regime.

Scan this QR code for any timely updates from the city of Miami on the park.

The Sacred Ceiba Tree

Between SW 10th St and Calle Ocho a striking ceiba tree with gnarled roots and spindly branches holds deep spiritual significance. Central to Afro-Cuban Santería, the tree is believed to connect the living with their ancestors.

Walk Little Havana

Little Havana is the Cuban cultural heart of Miami. The neighborhood pulses with music, art and history, essentially feeling like a portal straight to Cuba without having to leave the US. Find yourself immersed in a world of *cafecitos*, cigars and domino games while visiting the historic landmarks and cafes along the way.

START	END	LENGTH
Máximo Gómez Park	Café La Trova	0.6mi; 2 hours

1 A Walk in the Park

The soul of Little Havana, **Máximo Gómez Park** (p100; also known as Domino Park) buzzes with lively chatter and the clinking of dominoes. This epicenter of friendly competition is where locals gather daily to play domino matches. Colorful murals celebrating Cuban heritage are scattered throughout the park. Take in the sights and sounds of Cuba right in Miami.

2 You Can't Stop the Beat

No trip to Little Havana would be complete without a stop at the historic nightclub with a past as colorful as its neon sign. **Ball & Chain** (p98) is an iconic venue, with jazz legends such as Billie Holiday and Count Basie having graced its stage in the past. Today, you can strap on your dancing shoes, join a salsa lesson, grab a cocktail and enjoy some of the best live music in Miami.

3 Sweet Surrender

The sweetest way to fuel a walking adventure is with a heaping helping of ice cream and you won't find a better scoop than **Azucar Ice Cream**, where Cuban flavors take center stage. Their signature Abuela Maria – a mix of vanilla, guava, cream cheese and Maria cookies – is a must. Be sure to snap a pic out front where the giant ice cream cone is downright Instagrammable.

4 Reach for the Stars

Stroll along **Calle Ocho's Walk of Fame**, where literal stars along the sidewalk honor legendary Latin figures like Celia Cruz and Gloria Estefan. This Cuban twist on Hollywood Boulevard celebrates Latin musicians, actors and cultural icons. Don't keep your head down for too long though, the additional sights and sounds along Calle Ocho offer a multisensory experience.

5 Smoke Show

Discover the art of cigar-making at **Havana Classic Cigars**, where skilled *torcedores* (cigar rollers) craft cigars by hand. Here you will learn about the history and significance of cigars in Cuban culture as you watch the masters at work. If you are a cigar enthusiast, be sure to take home an authentic Cuban-style smoke.

6 Satiate & Caffeinate

For a truly authentic Little Havana experience pop over to one of Little Havana's most famous Cuban restaurants, **Café La Trova**. The menu features Cuban dishes with a contemporary take by James Beard Award-winning chef, Michelle Bernstein. If you aren't up for a full meal, no sweat! The establishment has a *ventanita* (a *cafecito* window) where you can order a Cuban coffee to go.

EXPERIENCES

Jam to Cuban Beats at Cubaocho

NIGHTLIFE

MAP: 1 P94 D3

Part art gallery, part music venue and part cultural research center, **Cubaocho** *(cubaocho.co)* is the beating heart of the Little Havana Art District. The space feels like an old Havana cigar bar, with walls covered in Cuban artwork that bridges the past and future. Its concerts feature top-tier Latin bands, drawing an eclectic crowd of music lovers and art enthusiasts alike. Whether you're sipping a fine rum or admiring the curated gallery, Cubaocho is a dive into Cuban culture. Arrive early to snag a good spot; live shows fill up fast.

Take in a Cocktail (or Three) & Show at Café La Trova

NIGHTLIFE

MAP: 2 P94 F3

If you're craving the glamour of 1950s Havana, **Café La Trova** *(cafelatrova.com)* takes you back. With its warm wood accents, well-dressed bartenders and faded Cuban decor, the space oozes vintage charm. Live bands play classic Cuban dance music, and the crowd – decked out in dresses and *guayaberas* – keeps the energy high. The cocktails, crafted by award-winning bartenders, are just as legendary as the music. Pro tip: order a daiquiri and be ready to dance – this place lets loose.

Ball & Chain: Salsa & Street Party Vibes

NIGHTLIFE

MAP: 3 P94 C3

A Little Havana institution, **Ball & Chain** *(ballandchainmiami.com)* is where the party never stops. Music spills onto Calle Ocho all day, and by night the salsa dancing often takes over the street. The historic venue, a jazz hot spot in the 1930s, still delivers top-notch live performances in a lively, tropical setting. Whether you're swinging to live Latin jazz, sipping a mojito or jumping into a spontaneous dance

A DECO SURPRISE

Think all the best South Florida deco is in South Beach? Visit the Tower Theater on Calle Ocho and think again. This renovated 1926 landmark features a proud deco facade and a beautifully restored interior. In its heyday the theater was the heart of Little Havana's social scene, serving as a bridge between the immigrant community and American pop culture through its film screenings. Today it continues that legacy by showcasing independent and Spanish-language films, sometimes both at once. The lobby frequently hosts art exhibitions, adding to its cultural significance. More than just a theater, it remains a beloved neighborhood anchor, a landmark generations have grown up with – and fought to preserve.

Ball & Chain

circle, it's always a good time. Visit during happy hour – typically 4-7pm on weekdays – for great deals and a more relaxed vibe before the late-night frenzy kicks in.

Yes, Eat Some Thai in Little Havana

FOOD & DRINK

In Little Havana you can take a trip around the Spanish-speaking world in just a few blocks. And we do mean the world – Cuban cuisine is only a small slice of Little Havana's pan-Latin palate. Menus span el Sud from Ecuador to El Salvador and Mexico to Mendoza, Argentina. While locals insist the best *comida latina* (Latin food) lies beyond Calle Ocho, you'll rarely go wrong stepping into any ethnic eatery in this part of town.

You don't even need to stick to the Western Hemisphere. Take **Lung Yai Thai Tapas** (MAP: 4 P94 B3; *lungyai.com*), a gem that proves sharing small plates on a humid afternoon isn't just a Spanish tradition. (By the way, the chicken wings here will blow your mind.)

For the ultimate Miami refreshment, grab a fresh juice or *batido* (milkshake) from **Los Pinareños Frutería** (MAP: 5 P94 D3) a beloved fruit stand. Sip a *guarapo* (sugarcane juice) while roosters cluck and locals gossip in Cuban-accented Spanish – this is as Miami as it gets, short of starring in a Pitbull song.

Circle Friday on the Calendar for Viernes Culturales

EVENTS

MAP: 6 P94 D3

Every third Friday of the month, from noon until late, **Viernes Culturales** *(Cultural Fridays; viernesculturales.org)* transforms the streets of Little Havana into a vibrant celebration of art, music and culture. The event features live music on stage, galleries open until 11pm, and a lively showcase of the neighborhood's creativity and joie de vivre.

The action unfolds in the Little Havana Historic District, between SW 15th and 17th Aves along Calle Ocho, where visitors can see cigar rollers, local arts and crafts for sale, and plenty of music and dancing under the stars.

Since its launch in 2000, Viernes Culturales has drawn thousands of revelers each month. Come with the right mindset – ready for a very good time – and you'll fit right into the mix.

Watch Some Dominoes (& Play if You Dare)

ACTIVITIES

Perhaps Little Havana's most evocative reminder of Cuban street life, **Máximo Gómez Park** (MAP: 7 P94 **D3**; *miami.gov; free entry*), more commonly called Domino Park, is a tree-shaded, gated oasis along Calle Ocho. The iron gates open daily from 9am to 6pm, welcoming regulars from across Miami. Here, competitive banter and strategizing unfold over games of dominoes, accompanied by cups of strong Cuban coffee.

The clack-clack of slapping tiles mixes with the sound of seasoned players trash-talking, while tourists snapping photos adds an amusing contrast – not that the players seem to mind. If anything, they feed off the crowd's energy. The air is thick with the scent of cigars, and a vivid mural depicting the 1994 Summit of the Americas enhances the atmosphere.

You might stop by for a few minutes or find yourself drawn into watching a game for longer. Domino-inspired tiles line the walkways and shaded benches offer a perfect spot to soak it all in. **Azucar Ice Cream** (MAP: 8 P94 **C3**; *azucaricecream.com*), a neighborhood favorite, is right across the street, if all the spectating makes you hungry.

Rub Elbows with the Locals at Versailles

PEOPLE-WATCHING

MAP: 9 P94 **A4**

Few Little Havana sights make the stomach rumble like the green-and-white sign of **Versailles** (*versaillesrestaurant.com*). The self-proclaimed 'most famous Cuban restaurant in the world' (a claim that's hard to dispute) has been a Miami institution since 1971.

Generations of Cuban Americans and Miami's Latin political elite gather in its dining room, sharing plates of black beans, *ropa vieja*, *croquetas* and countless cups of sweet, strong Cuban coffee. While the staples are all here, the menu also features regional Cuban dishes, including seafood paella, shredded dry beef (a drier alternative to *ropa vieja*) and grilled liver steak.

For a quick caffeine fix, stop by La Ventanita, the restaurant's walk-up window, where locals grab shot-like Cuban coffees called *cortaditos* and *coladas*.

LISTINGS

Best Places for...

$ Budget $$ Midrange $$$ Top End

Eating

Cuban Food

Old's Havana Cuban Bar & Cocina $$

10 D3

Snag a table in the pretty tropical garden of this hot spot to feast on *picadillo*, *ropa vieja* and *vaca frita* (shredded beef with lime). *11am-11pm*

Sala'o Cuban Restaurant & Bar $$

 C3

With live music every night, this favorite serves specialties like *rabo encendido* (oxtail). *hours vary*

Sanguich Little Havana $

12 A3

A cult-favorite neighborhood spot where gourmet takes on classic Cuban sandwiches have people lining up. *10am–6pm*

Small Plates

Xixón $$

13 A4

A modern Spanish tapas joint with excellent *bacalao* (cod) fritters, sizzling shrimp and baby eel. *xixonspanishrestaurant.com, noon-10pm*

Seafood

La Camaronera Seafood Joint $$

14 A1

Famous for *pan con minuta*, a fried fish sandwich, served inside soft Cuban bread. *lacamaronera.com, 11:30am-5:30pm*

Drinking

Coffee

La Colada Gourmet

15 C3

Specialty coffee spot offering the best Cuban brews in town. *lacoladagourmet.com, 10am-10pm*

Macondo Coffee Roasters

 A4

A stylish coffee shop with a Latin American influence. *macondocoffee.com, hours vary*

Cocktails

Guantanamera Café and Lounge

17 D3

A laid-back spot with cigars, cocktails and live Latin music. *guantanameracigars.com, hours vary*

Bar Nancy

18 A3

A nautical-themed bar with live music, creative cocktails and a local crowd. *nancy305.com, hours vary*

Shopping

Cuban Classics

Havana Collection Experience

19 D3

One of the best collections of classic *guayaberas* in Miami. Prices are higher, but the quality ensures long-lasting wear. *11am-5pm*

Little Havana Cigar Factory

20 C3

A must-visit for cigar aficionados, offering a selection of premium Cuban-style cigars. *littlehavanacigars.com, 10am-7pm Mon-Sat, to 6pm Sun*

See p114 for eating, drinking and shopping listings

Explore Coconut Grove

Coconut Grove has always been a little different from the rest of Miami. Established in the late 1800s by Bahamian settlers, artists and pioneers, it grew into a bohemian retreat, attracting free spirits, musicians and intellectuals throughout the 20th century. Its lush setting and waterfront location fostered a relaxed, village-like atmosphere that remains today. Over the years, development brought upscale residences and a thriving commercial core, but the Grove has retained its laid-back and artsy character. Wandering its streets, you'll find a mix of historic homes, modern condos and a deep connection to Miami's maritime roots.

Getting Around

Walking

Flat terrain makes Coconut Grove perfect for exploring on foot. The heart of the Grove, centered around CocoWalk and Main Hwy, is pedestrian-friendly with shaded sidewalks.

Buses

The number 22 bus runs through the Grove, taking Tigertail Ave and SW 27th Ave to the Coconut Grove Metrorail Station. From there, you can connect to the Metrorail or catch the free Coconut Grove trolley to key spots.

Bicycles

Several Citi Bike kiosks make cycling easy. Downtown Miami is just 5 miles away, offering a scenic ride via South Bayshore Dr.

THE BEST

ESTATE TOUR Vizcaya Museum & Gardens (p105)

GARDENS Kampong (p110)

PARK Barnacle Historic State Park (p111)

CHURCH WITH A VIEW Ermita de la Caridad (p113)

SHOPPING STROLL CocoWalk (p113)

Ermita de la Caridad (p113)
PISAPHOTOGRAPHY/SHUTTERSTOCK

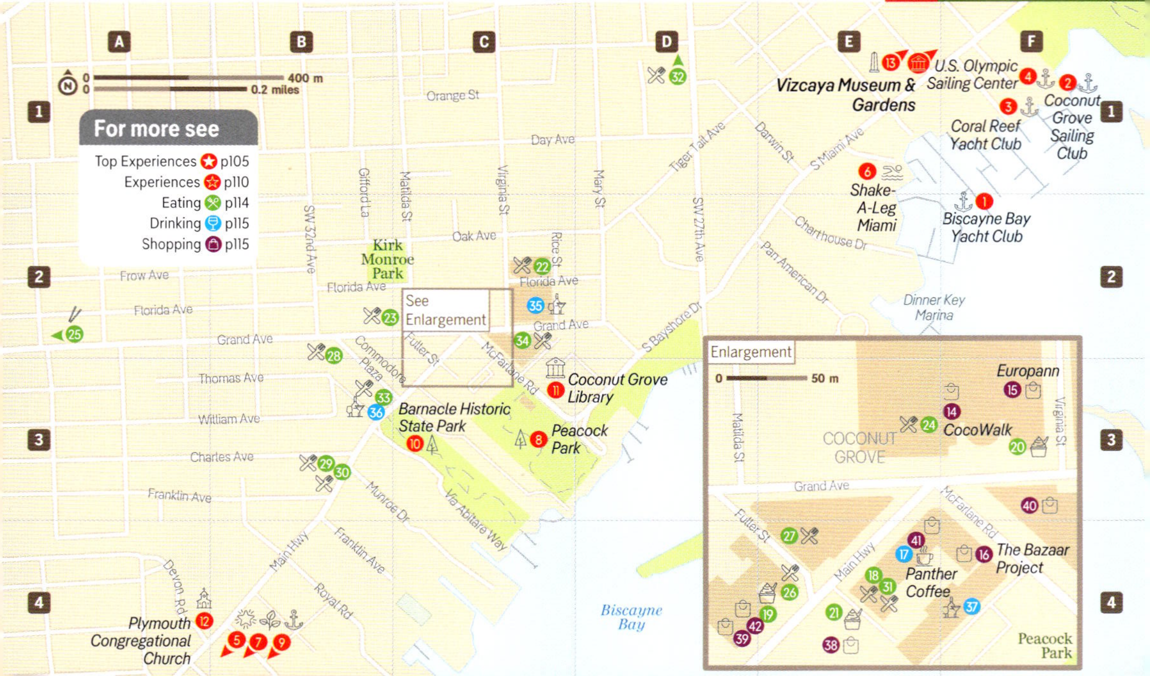

A
B
C
D
E
F
1
2
3
4
0 400 m
0 0.2 miles
For more see
Top Experiences p105
Experiences p110
Eating p114
Drinking p115
Shopping p115
Orange St
Day Ave
Tiger Tail Ave
Darwin St
S Miami Ave
Vizcaya Museum & Gardens
U.S. Olympic Sailing Center
Coral Reef Yacht Club
Coconut Grove Sailing Club
Shake-A-Leg Miami
Biscayne Bay Yacht Club
Charthouse Dr
Pan American Dr
Dinner Key Marina
Gifford La
Matilda St
Virginia St
Mary St
SW 27th Ave
SW 32nd Ave
Oak Ave
Rice St
Kirk Monroe Park
Frow Ave
Florida Ave
Grand Ave
See Enlargement
S Bayshore Dr
Commodore Plaza
Fuller St
McFarlane Rd
Coconut Grove Library
Thomas Ave
William Ave
Barnacle Historic State Park
Peacock Park
Charles Ave
Franklin Ave
Munroe Dr
Via Abitare Way
Main Hwy
Royal Rd
Devon Rd
Plymouth Congregational Church
Biscayne Bay
Enlargement
0 50 m
Europann
CocoWalk
COCONUT GROVE
Grand Ave
McFarlane Rd
The Bazaar Project
Panther Coffee
Peacock Park

★ TOP EXPERIENCE

Vizcaya Museum & Gardens

They call Miami the Magic City and, if it is, this Italian villa, the housing equivalent of a Fabergé egg, is its most fairy-tale-like residence. Perched over the water, Vizcaya *(vizcaya.org; adult/child $25/10)* is a fascinating place to wander, with art-filled rooms, lavish antique furniture and picturesque gardens.

MAP P104 **E1**

A Gilded Age Dream

Back in 1916 industrialist James Deering kicked off a Miami tradition: making a fortune and then building an absurdly grand estate. He spared no expense, hiring 1000 workers – 10% of the local population at the time – to construct his Mediterranean Revival masterpiece. The Coconut Grove mansion, fronting Biscayne Bay, was inspired by European palaces and filled with Renaissance-era furniture, tapestries and artwork. The largest space, the informal living room, is often called the 'Renaissance Hall' for its collection of 14th- to 17th-century masterpieces. Nearby, the music room dazzles with wall canvases imported from northern Italy, while the banquet hall's regal furnishings transport visitors straight into a European imperial feast.

Every room at Vizcaya feels like stepping into a different era. Deering's vision blended old-world grandeur with the latest 20th-century innovations; this lavish retreat had state-of-the-art plumbing, electricity and even a telephone system. The library, filled with leather-bound tomes, evokes the spirit of a European scholar's study, while the ornate bedrooms, with their elaborate canopies and antique furnishings, feel fit for royalty.

PLANNING TIP
The complex hosts a farmers market every Sunday from 9am to 2pm, with local vendors aplenty selling everything from hand-crafted goods to fresh-picked fruits to baked goods.

Scan this QR Code to purchase tickets to the grounds.

MANAMANA/SHUTTERSTOCK

Even the kitchen, with its early appliances, showcases the mansion's forward-thinking design. Though Miami has transformed dramatically since Deering's time, Vizcaya remains a time capsule of Gilded Age opulence.

QUICK BREAK
Doggi's Arepa Bar, north of the complex, is a Miami favorite for Venezuelan morsels, burgers and, yes, massive, stuffed arepa concoctions.

Secret Gardens & a Stairway to the Sky

If the Main House is Vizcaya's heart, its gardens are the soul. Modeled on the grand formal gardens of 17th- and 18th-century Italy, they contrast beautifully with the untamed mangroves beyond. Walking through these green spaces is like meandering through an aristocrat's European fantasy. Sculptures and fountains punctuate the landscape, while vine-covered walls add a touch of mystery. The Garden Mound, an elevated terrace, offers one of the best views of the estate's sprawling greenery.

The gardens unfold like a series of outdoor rooms, each with its own personality. There's the intimate Secret Garden with delicate pathways and stone benches, the playful Maze Garden with its twisting hedges, the classical Theater Garden and the once-aquatic Fountain Garden. Every turn reveals a new perspective, a hidden statue or a romantic alcove – no wonder the estate has long been a favorite backdrop for weddings and photo shoots. Beyond the manicured gardens, Deering preserved native hardwood hammocks, ensuring that part of Miami's original landscape remained untouched.

One of the property's most intriguing elements is at the waterfront: a stone barge designed as a decorative breakwater. This sculpted structure, shaped like a Venetian ship, not only protected Vizcaya from waves but also served as an extravagant setting for parties. From here the view of Biscayne Bay is spectacular, with the Miami skyline shimmering in the distance.

Making the Most of It

A visit to Vizcaya Museum & Gardens isn't a quick stop – it's an immersive experience. Give yourself at least a few hours to explore the house and wander the gardens at a leisurely pace. The estate opens at 9:30am, and arriving early means fewer crowds and cooler temperatures for strolling outside. The museum is closed on Tuesdays.

Parking is free, and while Vizcaya is accessible by car, it's also an easy trip via public transport – the nearby Vizcaya Metrorail Station makes it convenient from Downtown Miami.

A HOLLYWOOD FAVORITE

Vizcaya's cinematic charm makes it a popular filming location. Movies like Iron *Man 3*, *Bad Boys II* and *Ace Ventura: Pet Detective* have all featured scenes shot within its lavish estate and gardens.

DEERING'S UNFINISHED VISION

James Deering originally planned for Vizcaya to include a village with staff quarters, workshops and greenhouses. While only some of it was completed, remnants of this ambitious expansion still exist today.

Walk Coconut Grove

Tree-lined streets, outdoor cafes and pretty waterfront green spaces give Miami's oldest neighborhood a village-like vibe. Its compact center is more walkable than many other parts of Miami, which is a big draw for many residents. Grove folk would agree: strolling among its one-of-a-kind boutiques and watering holes is one of the best ways to spend a sunny afternoon.

START	END	LENGTH
Barnacle Historic State Park	Peacock Park	1 mile; 3 hours

Matilda St
Virginia St
Rice St
Grand Ave
Fuller St
Main Hwy
Commodore Plaza
McFarlane Rd
COCONUT GROVE
S Bayshore Dr
Myres Bayside Park
Via Abitare Way
START
END
0
100 m

1 Pioneer History

Step back in time at **Barnacle Historic State Park** (p111), where Miami's oldest home still stands in its original position. The house was built by pioneer Ralph Munroe, one of Coconut Grove's first snowbirds. The 5-acre park is a shady oasis, perfect for a stroll, and even has some prime bird-watching opportunities despite its urban location. Guided tours of the house are available for a small fee.

2 Caffeine Boost

One of South Florida's favorite specialty coffee roasters, **Panther Coffee** (p113), has an outpost in Coconut Grove. Their carefully crafted, single-origin brews are a beloved treat for locals and travelers alike. The laid-back vibes of this location makes for a perfect spot to relax along the journey and soak in the Grove's charm.

3 Tropical Elegance

Mayfair House & Garden is an architectural wonder. Originally designed by Kenneth Treister in 1985, the hotel was recently renovated by Goodrich, reopening in 2022. The hotel was carefully transformed with the original integrity of the artistic design in mind. The property features lush greenery, and artwork and photography that embody Bahamian folk art traditions.

4 Go Do-Nuts

Miami is no stranger to creative culinary endeavors, and that is no different for the breakfast pastry scene. Miami-based **Salty Donut** recently opened its Coconut Grove location with no shortage of indulgent doughnut choices. The maple and bacon doughnut – made with a 24-hour brioche and topped with in-house candied bacon – is memorable.

5 Serene Stopover

Feel the city melt away with a glass of wine in a lush patio setting that feels more like a secret garden than a restaurant. Nestled in Peacock Park, **Glass & Vine's** extensive wine menu and locally sourced plates will satisfy any taste buds. Sit back, relax and enjoy the atmosphere and good company.

6 Urban Oasis

A final Coconut Grove green space set to wow you is **Peacock Park** (p110). Take a walk along the shaded paths or find a quiet moment to reflect at the meditation garden. Find a little piece of history at the oldest marked gravesite in the city of Miami, the original gravesite of Eva Munroe. The waterfront park also has a boardwalk along the water where you can see hordes of sailboats in Biscayne Bay.

EXPERIENCES

Set Sail or Learn How To

OUTDOOR ACTIVITIES

Many a salty dog has set sail from Coconut Grove, aka the sailing capital of Miami, for waypoints in the Caribbean and well, well beyond. And all it takes is a stroll around the sail-centric spots clustered close together here – **Biscayne Bay Yacht Club** (MAP: 1 P104 F2; *biscaynebayyachtclub.com*), **Coconut Grove Sailing Club** (MAP: 2 P104 F1; *cgsc.org*), **Coral Reef Yacht Club** (MAP: 3 P104 F1; *coralreefyachtclub.org*) and the **U.S. Olympic Sailing Center** (MAP: 4 P104 F1; *usasailingcentermiami.org*), among them – to feel the wind in your virtual sails and perhaps spark a desire to get out on the water, too.

For that, happily, you have options. Consider setting sail on guided tours aboard pontoon boats with the **Biscayne National Park Institute** (MAP: 5 P104 B4; *biscaynenationalparkinstitute.org; prices vary*) from Dinner Key Marina in Coconut Grove to snorkel patch reefs and shipwrecks within Biscayne National Park. Other boat trips on offer from the institute include historic tours to Boca Chita Key, just offshore, and Stiltsville. **Shake-A-Leg Miami** (MAP: 6 P104 E1; *shakealegmiami.org*) is a noble and civic-minded water sports center that provides activities for people with physical, developmental and economic challenges.

Enter a Wild World of Color at the Kampong

GARDENS

MAP: 7 P104 B4

David Fairchild, the Indiana Jones of the botanical world and founder of Fairchild Tropical Botanic Garden (p120), would rest at the Kampong (Malay/Indonesian for 'village') between journeys all over the world, during which he sought beautiful and profitable plant life.

As a pioneer of tropical botany, Fairchild was no slouch when it came to his own tropical backyard back home in Miami. He and his wife bought the **Kampong** *(ntbg.org; tours $7-27)* as their winter residence on the shores of Biscayne Bay in Coconut Grove. Here they played host to notable guests like Thomas Edison, Henry Ford and Dwight Eisenhower.

Today, the Kampong and its lush gardens are listed on the National Register of Historic Places, while the fecund grounds serve as a classroom for the National Tropical Botanical Garden. Self-guided tours (allow at least an hour) are available by appointment, as are $27 one-hour guided tours. Keep an eye out for the peanut butter fruit (yes, that's real!), the fragrant ylang-ylang flower and the impressive jackfruit trees.

Park It at Peacock Park

RECREATION

MAP: 8 P104 C3

City parks always provide a window into the true pulse of a neighborhood, and Coconut Grove's beloved **Peacock Park** *(miami.gov; free entry)* is no exception. Extending down to the edge of Biscayne Bay and open from 7am to 10pm daily, it serves as the great open backyard of Coconut Grove.

Young families stop by the playground, joggers and power walkers take in the view along the waterfront, and sports lovers join the action on the ball fields. In fact, the boardwalk trail that runs by the bay offers some of the cleanest, most peaceful views of Biscayne Bay on the mainland side.

What's in a name? You'd think gaudy birds roamed the grounds, but no. This 9-acre plot was once the site of the Bayview Inn, owned by Charles and Isabella Peacock (she later renamed it the Peacock Inn). The Peacocks employed Black Bahamian workers, who arrived via Key West to Miami and formed the core of the oldest Black community in Miami. The knowledge they brought from the islands – about tropical plants, agriculture and building in this environment – became essential to the development of Coconut Grove.

WHAT'S FOR 'DINNER'

Nestled just north of Peacock Park and on the shores of Biscayne Bay, Dinner Key was once a US Navy air station and then Pan Am's seaplane base in the 1930s. It's now one of South Florida's largest marinas, lined with sailboats and yachts. The **marina** is a popular launching point for trips into Biscayne Bay, with boat charters available. Dinner Key Picnic Islands Park also looms right offshore where, yes, you can have a scenic picnic. As for that historic Pan Am terminal, it still stands – it's morphed into Miami City Hall.

MAP: 9 P104 **B4**

Catch a Show & Miami's Oldest Residence in One

PARK

MAP: 10 P104 **C3**

At the center of Coconut Grove village sits Miami-Dade County's oldest residence – the former home of pioneer Ralph Munroe, Miami's first honorable snowbird. You can come for a picnic or one of the regularly scheduled concerts on the grounds of **Barnacle Historic State Park** *(thebarnacle.org; entry $2)*. Built in 1891, this 5-acre park – which Munroe originally bought for just $400 (imagine!) – is a shady oasis ideal for strolling and a great spot for kids to run off some energy. The home's name comes from its irregularly shaped rooms, including one in the form of an octagon.

Munroe's boat-building expertise influenced his home's unique design, incorporating elements of traditional Caribbean architecture. His engineering skills have stood the test of time – the Barnacle has survived major hurricanes, including Hurricane Andrew.

JOHNNY MICHAEL/SHUTTERSTOCK

Barnacle Historic State Park (p111)

The Barnacle hosts frequent events, from sailing regattas to moonlight concerts featuring jazz and classical music. As far as outdoor venues for this sort of chilled-out music go, this place is just chef's kiss.

Find Eva Munroe's Grave SIGHT

MAP: 11 P104 C3

Completed in 1963 the **Coconut Grove Library** *(mdpls.org)* has limestone walls and a steep roof, paying homage to the original 1901 library that once stood here. Inside you'll find a small, well-curated reference section on South Florida. Just outside, tucked into a small gated area, lies the humble headstone of Eva Munroe, who passed away in 1882. Hers is the oldest known American grave in Miami-Dade County.

A sad historical footnote: local African American settlers died before Eva, but their deaths were never officially recorded. Her husband, Ralph Munroe, was so devastated by her passing that he threw himself into his life's most ambitious project – building the Barnacle, now the oldest home in the area.

Visit the Striking Plymouth Congregational Church CHURCH

MAP: 12 P104 A4

Dating to 1917 the **Plymouth Congregational Church** *(plymouthmiami.org)* in Coconut Grove is one of the most striking houses of worship in Miami, from its solid masonry to a hand-carved door from a Pyrenean monastery that looks like it should be kicked in by Antonio Banderas carrying a guitar case full of explosives, Salma Hayek on his arm.

That's all to say: even in a city blessed with many fine Spanish Mission–style churches, architecturally this is an exceptional example. The church opens rarely, though all (and truly all – this is an LGBTQ+ friendly congregation) are welcome at the organ- and choir-led 10am Sunday service.

Pack a Picnic for this Cuban Church Icon

CHURCH

MAP: 13 P104 E1

The Catholic diocese purchased bayfront land from Deering's villa Vizcaya estate and built a shrine here for its displaced Cuban parishioners. Built in 1967 **Ermita de la Caridad** *(ermita.org)* is a beacon facing the homeland 290 miles due south, as well as a lighthouse for Miamians who long for a land they may never have visited.

This isn't the only way this church – full title: Santuario Nacional de Nuestra Señora de la Caridad – engages with Cuba. A mural inside depicts the island's history, and a Spanish-language presence is the norm for the congregation. Outside, a grassy stretch of waterfront makes a fine spot for a picnic.

Stroll & Shop at CocoWalk

SHOPPING

Coconut Grove has evolved into one of Miami's most stylish shopping hubs, and nowhere is this more apparent than at **CocoWalk** (MAP: 14 P104 **F3**; *cocowalk.com*). This open-air mall-meets-town-square is a mix of local boutiques, indie brands and upscale national retailers, all under palms and within a laid-back stretch.

For something coastal, pop in **Europann** (MAP: 15 P104 **F3**; *europann-usa.com*), a St Tropez-bred men's boutique filled with chic and beach-y wear. Over at **The Bazaar Project** (MAP: 16 P104 **F4**; *thebazaarproject.com)* you'll find statement home decor and jewelry that feel more like modern art than souvenirs.

CocoWalk's breezy courtyards and sidewalk cafes make it tempting to linger. Pro tip: grab a coffee from nearby **Panther Coffee** (MAP: 17 P104 **E4**; *panthercoffee.com*) and people-watch from a shaded perch. If you're here on a weekend, expect a lively atmosphere, with live music and an influx of stylish locals sipping cocktails between shopping sprees.

A 'MERRIE CHRISTMAS'

Despite its holiday-themed name, Merrie Christmas Park on the southwest edge of Coconut Grove isn't about Santa or snow. It's named after Merrie Christmas Wood, a Miami philanthropist who donated the land for public use. This quiet, tree-shaded park is a peaceful retreat from the area's broader hum. Kids love the playground, while locals bring blankets for a lazy afternoon under the massive oaks – consider this an under-the-radar picnic spot. If Fido is traveling with you, leashed dogs are welcome.

LISTINGS

Best Places for...

See p104 for map of locations

$ Budget $$ Midrange $$$ Top End

Eating

Sweets & Treats

Fireman Derek's Bake Shop $
18 E4
Killer key lime pie, coconut guava rum cake, empanadas and more draw sweet-tooth types. *firemandereks.com, hours vary*

Danielle Gelato $
19 E4
Artisan gelato tempts your taste buds with pistachio, passion fruit and more. *daniellegelato.com, noon-11pm*

Salt & Straw $
20 F3
Small-batch ice creams with lots of vegan offerings star. Don't miss the freckled mint chocolate chip with coconut undertones. *saltandstraw.com, noon-midnight Mon-Fri, from 11am Sat & Sun*

Morelia Ice Cream Paletas $
21 E4
This local chain's gourmet pops are kosher and made with natural ingredients. *paletasmorelia.com, hours vary*

Vegetarian Friendly

Bombay Darbar $$
22 C2
One of Miami's best-loved Indian restaurants, serving richly spiced curries, tandoori dishes and buttery naan in a lively setting. *bombaydarbar.com, hours vary*

Last Carrot $

B2
This unpretentious vegetarian cafe has been dishing out fresh, healthy wraps, sandwiches and smoothies since the 1970s. *thelastcarrot.getsauce.com, 10am-7pm Mon-Sat*

PLANTA Queen $$

E3
This bright, beautiful queen is a vegan's dream, serving plant-based Asian-inspired fare. *plantarestaurants.com, hours vary*

Casual

Matsuri $$

A2
Miami doesn't want for trendy sushi spots, but this strip-mall hideaway trades in the real deal. *matsurimiami.com, hours vary*

Chug's Diner $$
26 E4
Mix an American diner and a Cuban cafeteria and you've got Chug's, serving things like short rib *boliche* (pot roast) and cast-iron pancakes. *chugsdiner.com, hours vary*

Burgers & Beer

Barracuda Taphouse & Grill $$
27 E4
You'll never go wrong with a snapper or grouper sandwich at this beloved spot. *hours vary*

LoKal $$

B2
Hits the spot when you just want a damn good craft beer and burger in a good-vibes-only setting. *kushhospitality.com, 11:30am-10pm Sun-Tue, to 11pm Wed-Sat*

Taurus $$

B3
Cool mix of wood paneling, smoky leather chairs, about 100 beers to choose from and a convivial vibe. *thetauruscoconutgrove.com, 5pm-3am*

Worthy Splurges

Ariete $$$

30 B3

Michelin star-recipient merging Latin traditions and French techniques. *arietecoconutgrove.com, 5:30-11pm*

Los Félix $$$

31 E4

The maize is ground daily at this Mexican spot, where the menu is inspired by indigenous traditions. *los felixmiami.com, hours vary*

Breakfast

Berries in the Grove $$

32 D1

A relaxed neighborhood favorite serving generous portions of omelets, pancakes and healthy smoothies. *berriesin thegrove.com, 7am-10pm*

GreenStreet Cafe $$

33 B3

A true Coconut Grove institution known for its all-day brunch, massive cinnamon rolls and strong mimosas. *greenstreetcafe. net, 7am-midnight*

Carrot Express $

34 C2

Beloved health-forward regional chain with an expansive all-day break-fast menu, juice selections and more – make sure to snag a massive cookie to-go. *carrotexpress.com, 7am-9pm*

Drinking

Rooftop Retreats

Sipsip Rum Bar

35 C2

Sipsip celebrates the Grove's Caribbean heritage with island-inspired cocktails and bites. *mayfairhousemiami.com, 11am-10pm*

Level 6 Rooftop

36 B3

Impeccable scenery, curated music, Spanish plates and perfected cocktails with Biscayne Bay views. *level6miami. com, 4pm-midnight*

Bellini

37 F4

Atop the Mr C hotel, Bellini is a swanky rooftop Italian restaurant and bar serving coastal dishes with sky-high views. *bellinirestaurant.com, 7am-10pm*

Shopping

Fashion

Palm Produce Resortwear

38 E4

A go-to for classic Miami resort fashion, offering lightweight linen, colorful prints and laid-back yet polished vacation staples. *palmproduceresortwear. com, 10am-7pm Mon-Sat, 11am-6pm Sun*

Agua Bendita

39 D4

Colombian artisanship meets high-fashion swimwear at this boutique known for its bold bikinis and breezy cover-ups. *agua bendita.com, 11am-7pm*

Alice + Olivia

40 F3

Bright, playful and always on-trend, this designer boutique serves up state-ment-making women's fashion. *aliceandolivia. com, 10am-7pm*

Books & Gifts

Books & Books

41 E4

Miami's beloved indie bookstore chain brings a literary escape to the Grove, with bestsellers, indie gems and a cozy space for book lovers. *booksandbooks.com, 10am-9pm*

Celestial Treasures

42 D4

A mystical haven for crystals, tarot cards and spiritual gifts, perfect for those seeking cosmic energy and good vibes. *celestial-treasures.com, 11am-7pm*

See p130
for eating, drinking and shopping listings

Explore Coral Gables

A pastel-hued paradise that feels a world apart from the rest of Miami. This meticulously planned city, inspired by Mediterranean villages, has banyan-lined streets, grand boulevards and a walkable core. World-loved boutiques and upscale eateries cluster along and near the famed Miracle Mile, while historic landmarks like the opulent Biltmore Hotel and the Venetian Pool (you have to see it to believe it!) add to the city's allure. A haven of lush gardens and elegant mansions, Coral Gables is a sophisticated escape where Old World meets modern luxury, making it one of South Florida's most enchanting nooks.

Getting Around

Walk

The charming Miracle Mile district and nearby streets are lined with shops and restaurants, making for an easy-meets-scenic stroll.

Metrorail

The University and Douglas Road Metrorail stations provide access to Coral Gables. From there, hop on the free Coral Gables Trolley, which offers two routes connecting key areas, including Downtown, Miracle Mile and Merrick Park.

Car

Driving is straightforward via SW 22nd St (Coral Way) or US-1. Metered street parking is widely available, along with garages near shopping and dining areas.

THE BEST

HOTEL WORTH A STAY & TOUR Biltmore Hotel (p126)

BUTTERFLY-FILLED STROLL Fairchild Tropical Botanic Garden (p120)

POOL LIKE YOU'VE NEVER SEEN Venetian Pool (p122)

FOR HISTORY BUFFS Coral Gables Museum (p127)

MANGROVE MOMENTS Matheson Hammock Park (p126)

Matheson Hammock Park (p126)
KATELYN RACANELLI/SHUTTERSTOCK

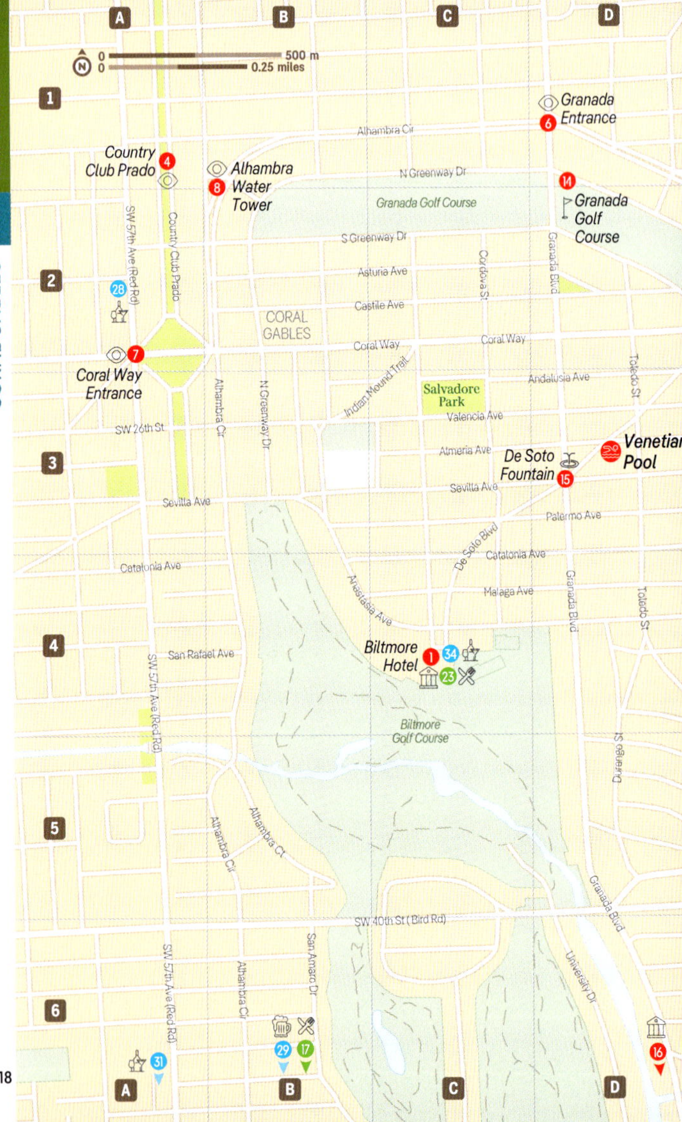
A
B
C
D
1
2
3
4
5
6
0 500 m
0 0.25 miles
Granada Entrance
6
Alhambra Cir
Country Club Prado
4
Alhambra Water Tower
8
N Greenway Dr
Granada Golf Course
14
Granada Golf Course
S Greenway Dr
SW 57th Ave (Red Rd)
Country Club Prado
Granada Blvd
Cordova St
Asturia Ave
28
Castile Ave
CORAL GABLES
Coral Way
Coral Way
7
Coral Way Entrance
Indian Mound Trail
Andalusia Ave
Toledo St
Salvadore Park
Alhambra Cir
N Greenway Dr
Valencia Ave
SW 26th St
Venetian Pool
Almeria Ave
De Soto Fountain
15
Sevilla Ave
Sevilla Ave
Palermo Ave
De Soto Blvd
Catalonia Ave
Catalonia Ave
Anastasia Ave
Malaga Ave
Granada Blvd
Toledo St
Biltmore Hotel
1
34
23
San Rafael Ave
SW 57th Ave (Red Rd)
Biltmore Golf Course
Duero St
Alhambra Cir
Alhambra Ct
Granada Blvd
SW 40th St (Bird Rd)
San Amaro Dr
Alhambra Cir
SW 57th Ave (Red Rd)
University Dr
29
17
31
16

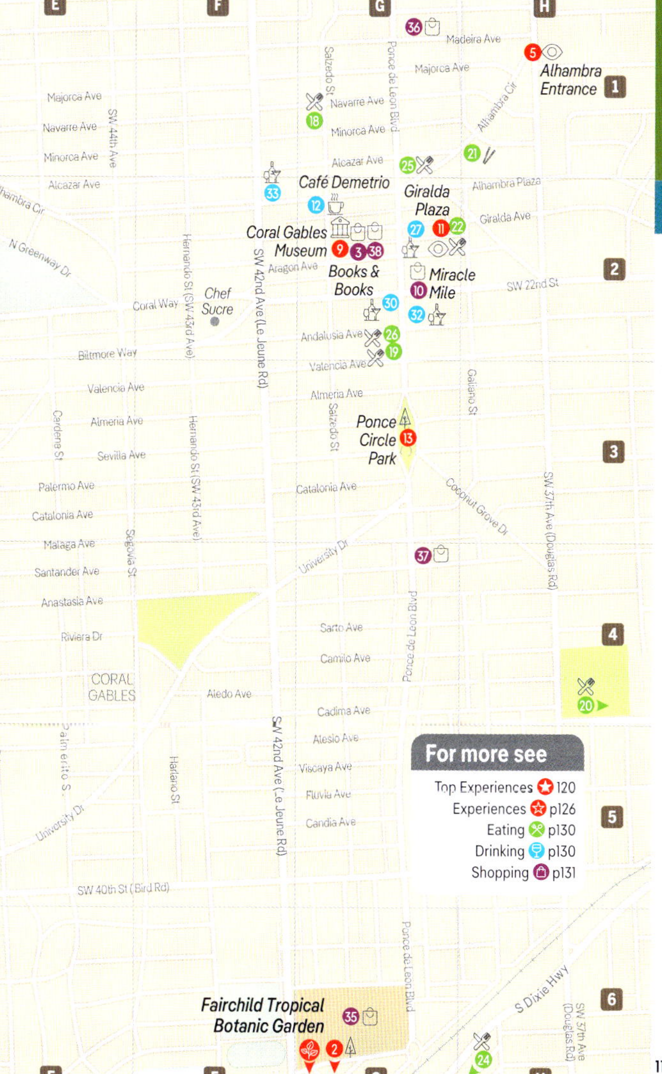

For more see
Top Experiences p120
Experiences p126
Eating p130
Drinking p130
Shopping p131

★ TOP EXPERIENCE

Fairchild Tropical Botanic Garden

The Fairchild is one of America's great tropical botanical gardens. A butterfly grove, tropical plant conservatory and gentle vistas of marsh and keys habitats, plus frequent art installations by artists such as Roy Lichtenstein, all contribute to the beauty of this peaceful, 83-acre garden.

MAP P118 **G6**

PLANNING TIP
You can score a discount by coming by bike, on foot or on public transit ($5 off each adult ticket, $2 off each child's ticket).

Scan this QR code for the scoop on its butterfly garden

A Tropical Wonderland

One of America's great botanical treasures, **Fairchild Tropical Botanic Garden** *(fairchild garden.org; adult/child $25/12)* is an 83-acre paradise where lush landscapes, rare plants and vibrant art installations create a serene escape. Founded in 1938 by businessman Robert Montgomery and named after explorer David Fairchild, the garden is a testament to plant conservation and tropical beauty. Meandering pathways lead through a butterfly grove, a tropical plant conservatory and sweeping marsh vistas. Frequent art installations – from Roy Lichtenstein sculptures to Dale Chihuly's glass work – add splashes of unexpected color, making a visit here as much about culture as it is about nature.

Wings of the Tropics

On-site, you can step into a kaleidoscope of color at Wings of the Tropics, where hundreds of butterflies flutter freely in a lush, tropical setting. Their iridescent wings catch the light as they dance between blooms, creating a magical spectacle. A behind-the-scenes highlight is the Vollmer Metamorphosis Lab, where visitors can watch in real time as butterflies emerge from their chrysalides. Several times a day, newly transformed butterflies

ALEKSANDR DYSKIN/SHUTTERSTOCK

are released into the exhibit, making each visit a moment of discovery. Ask a staff member when the next release is slated for – it will be worth the wait.

Living Art in the Garden

Amid the winding paths of the Tropical Plant Conservatory and the Rare Plant House, the *End of the Day Tower* rises like flickering flames from a tranquil pond. This striking Dale Chihuly glass sculpture glows with colorful tendrils, its base home to African cichlids that swim beneath its reflection. Nearby, the Richard H Simons Rainforest immerses visitors in a mini jungle, complete with a bubbling stream, waterfalls and orchids. Whether you come for the plants, the butterflies or the art, Fairchild is a quintessentially South Florida blend of nature and creativity.

QUICK BREAK
As culinary options are limited in this part of town, pop into the on-site Garden Restaurant for soups, sandwiches, salads and desserts with an organic flair.

★ TOP EXPERIENCE

Venetian Pool

There are pools and then there are pools, and you can leave it to Miami to serve up the latter on a silver platter. The Mediterranean Revival–style Venetian Pool *(coralgables.com, adult/child $22/17)* is one of the very few cool drinks of water that's listed on the National Register of Historic Places.

MAP P118 **D3**

PLANNING TIP
You need an admission ticket to access the pool. Tickets run $22 for adults and $17 for kids, so plan to spend some time here to get your money's worth.

Scan this QR code to purchase your admission ticket.

A Pool Born from a Quarry

The Venetian Pool, a one-of-a-kind aquatic paradise, came to life in 1924 as part of George Merrick's grand vision for Coral Gables. What began as a limestone quarry supplying stone for the city's Mediterranean-style buildings was transformed into a spectacular swimming destination through the efforts of Merrick, artist Denman Fink and architect Phineas Paist. To erase the unsightly scar left by excavation, they filled the pit with cool spring water, adorned it with mosaic tiles and surrounded it with lush landscaping. Originally dubbed the Venetian Casino, it quickly became a glamorous retreat for high society and Hollywood stars.

Grottoes, Waterfalls & a Swim Like No Other

The Venetian Pool isn't just big – it's 820,000 gallons of fresh water big, making it one of the largest freshwater pools in the country. Fed by underground aquifers, its crisp waters are drained and refilled regularly, keeping it refreshingly cool. The design is pure Mediterranean fantasy, with cascading waterfalls, Venetian-style moorings and a palm-fringed island. You can swim beneath the grand stone bridge, explore the shadowy rock caves or brave the 12ft grotto, a hidden cavern that feels like a secret escape. While there's no longer

WIRESTOCK CREATORS/SHUTTERSTOCK

an orchestra performing on the drained pool floor (yes, that was a thing), the ambience remains as enchanting as ever.

Pro Tips & Fun Facts

Venetian Pool recently reopened after renovations. Admission is limited daily, meaning you should arrive early to secure your spot. There's no chlorine here – the pool's natural water source is its best-kept secret. While depths range from 4ft to just over 8ft, families with little ones will appreciate the shallow 2ft kiddie area. Fun fact: once upon a time, gondolas floated across the pool, adding to its Venetian charm. Today, it remains a National Register of Historic Places landmark, ensuring its place as one of America's most unique swimming experiences.

QUICK BREAK

The Venetian Pool is nestled in a very residential area of Coral Gables. The closest cafe, **Chef Sucre**, is a 15-minute walk northeast, where draft beers and bistro fare await.

Walk Coral Gables

Coral Gables is where history, charm and Mediterranean flair meet in the most visually appetizing way. Walking through its Business Improvement District takes you through the heart of the commerce, dining and culture of the neighborhood. Along the way, you'll take in a statue honoring its founder, bustling shopping streets and cultural nooks.

START	END	LENGTH
Ponce Circle Park	Coral Gables City Hall	1 mile; 2 hours

1 A Man & His City

A fitting start to a walking tour of Coral Gables is **Ponce Circle Park** where a bronze statue of George Merrick, founder of the city, stands in honor of his vision to shape the area's Mediterranean Revival–style and planned community design. The park is surrounded by said architecture and is a top place to appreciate the designs.

2 Commerce & Culture

Anything your shop-a-holic heart desires can be found on **Miracle Mile** (p128). This section of Coral Way is the city's main street and has become one of South Florida's premiere shopping, dining and entertainment destinations. Its tree-lined streets are marked by outdoor cafes, boutiques and historical landmarks like the Miracle Theatre, which was built in 1948.

3 Pedestrians Only

The City Beautiful has no shortage of shopping and dining opportunities. Just off Miracle Mile lies **Giralda Plaza**, a pedestrian-only walkway lined with shops, restaurants, bars and art galleries. This district has slightly more historic charm than some of its neighboring counterparts. That charm especially radiates at night when string lights illuminate the streets, making for a very cozy and romantic atmosphere.

4 Book Nook

The best indie bookstore in South Florida has a location in Coral Gables and is a wonderful place to stock up on your beach reading material or see authors in action at one of its frequent in-store events. **Books & Books** (p126) has a cafe and restaurant, with dining on a quintessentially Coral Gables, Mediterranean-esque patio at the front of the shop.

5 Uncovering the City Beautiful

The **Coral Gables Museum** (p127) is a well-plotted introduction to the narrative of the founding and growth of Coral Gables. The collection includes historical artifacts and mementoes from succeeding generations in this eccentric little village. The main building is the old Coral Gables police and fire station; it's a lovely architectural blend of Coral Gables' Mediterranean flair and Miami Beach's muscular, depression-moderne style.

6 Civic Duty

Sure, it can be amusing to imagine the tedious grind of city council business being conducted within the grand, historic **City Hall** building, which opened in 1928. Its architecture suggests a sense of romance and power – lofty ideals that feel worlds apart from surely routine debates over parking ordinances and municipal regulations.

EXPERIENCES

Book a Tour (or Stay) at Biltmore Hotel

HISTORY & ARCHITECTURE

MAP: 1 P118 C4

In a city known for its flash, the **Biltmore Hotel** *(biltmorehotel.com)* exudes a timeless elegance that feels untouched by the decades. Sprawling across 150 acres in Coral Gables, this National Historic Landmark boasts lush tropical grounds, tennis courts, an 18-hole golf course and one of the most extravagant hotel pools in the country. You don't need to be a guest to appreciate its grandeur – free guided tours, offered Sundays at 2pm by the Dade Heritage Trust *(dadeheritagetrust.org; free entry)*, provide an inside look at its storied past.

Modeled after Seville's 12th-century Giralda Tower, the hotel's central spire dominates the skyline, while inside, soaring ceilings, Corinthian columns and hand-painted murals set the scene. Back in the day, a private canal system carried celebrity guests like Judy Garland and the Vanderbilts around by gondola. Though the waterways are gone, the lavish pool remains. As for ghosts? Some say mobster Fatty Walsh, gunned down on the 13th floor, still roams the hallways.

Matheson Hammock Park

NATURE & RECREATION

MAP: 2 P118 G6

The first park in Dade County and Miami's oldest, **Matheson Hammock Park** *(miamidade.gov; free entry)* is a 630-acre haven of banyan trees, palms and dense mangrove swamps, located just south of Coral Gables. It's a prime spot for nature lovers, with hungry raccoons, fragrant lawns and even the occasional alligator sighting. The park also features a marina and a sailing school, making it a hub for boaters and other water enthusiasts.

One of its most unique draws is the human-made atoll pool, a tidal lagoon that rises and falls with Biscayne Bay. A favorite swimming spot for local families, it offers calm, shallow waters perfect for young bathers. While exploring the trails or relaxing by the water, keep an eye out for wading birds and stunning bay views.

Peruse Titles Rare & Treasured at Books & Books

BOOKSTORE

MAP: 3 P118 G2

The most renowned indie bookstore in South Florida has branches across town, but the Coral Gables outpost of **Books & Books** *(booksandbooks.com)* is its flagship and a special sort of place. Think of the images that spring to mind when you imagine a wonderful old library, then place that temple of literature in the tropics and wash it with golden Miami sunshine.

We're not the only ones taken with this brick-and-mortar tribute to all things paper and ink – it feels like every writer who has ever visited Florida has crossed the store's stage. Books & Books was founded by Mitchell Kaplan, a teacher-turned-founder of Miami Book Fair International, an event that has no small presence at this store.

Gates to the City Beautiful

GATES

George Merrick planned a series of elaborate entry gates to Coral Gables, but a real estate bust meant that many projects went unfinished. It's a shame, as the gorgeous Gables deserves over-the-top entrances. On the other hand, the unfinished nature of the project adds a timeless atmosphere – or maybe speaks to humanity's hubris? Whatever the case, they look cool.

Among the completed gates worth seeing – many of which resemble (and are named for) the entrance pavilions to grand Spanish estates – are the **Country Club Prado** (MAP: 4 P118 **A1**), the **Alhambra Entrance** (MAP: 5 P118 **H1**), the **Granada Entrance** (MAP: 6 P118 **D1**) and the **Coral Way Entrance** (MAP: 7 P118 **A2**). Also notable is the **Alhambra Water Tower** (MAP: 8 P118 **B1**), where Greenway Crt and Ferdinand St meet Alhambra Circle, which resembles a Moorish lighthouse.

Go Gaga Over Gables History

MUSEUM

MAP: 9 P118 **G2**

Housed in a beautifully restored 1939 coral-stone building that once served as the city's police and fire stations, the **Coral Gables Museum** *(coralgablesmuseum.org; adult/child $15/5)* is dedicated to celebrating the history, architecture and planning of the 'City Beautiful.' Exhibits focus on urban design, historic preservation and the unique vision that shaped Coral Gables into one of South Florida's most picturesque communities.

BIRTH OF A BEAUTIFUL CITY

Coral Gables was born from the ambitious vision of developer George Merrick, who in the 1920s set out to create a 'City Beautiful' inspired by Mediterranean architecture and meticulous urban planning. Carved from Florida wilderness, the city was designed with grand entrances, tree-canopied streets and a focus on harmony between nature and architecture. Its strict building codes have preserved its aesthetic charm, making it one of Miami's most distinctive neighborhoods. Today, Coral Gables remains a model of thoughtful city design, blending historic elegance with contemporary vibrancy. It's a true upscale enclave where history and refinement converge.

Beyond the galleries, the museum offers guided walking and bike tours that highlight the city's Mediterranean Revival architecture and photo-worthy boulevards. The building itself is worth a visit – featuring a former jail cell, a serene courtyard and art deco-era details that nod to its past. Among the relics on display is the original alarm panel from the city's first firehouse, a glimpse into early firefighting technology. Another standout is an antique 1920s Coral Gables streetlamp, a reminder of George Merrick's meticulous city planning.

Stroll the Miracle Mile & Giralda Plaza

SHOPPING & DINING

The heart of Coral Gables beats along the **Miracle Mile** (MAP: 10 P118 G2), a vibrant stretch of shops, restaurants and galleries. Designed as a pedestrian-friendly district, it's a favorite for both locals and visitors looking to explore boutiques, sip coffee alfresco or dine at some of Miami's top restaurants.

Just off the Mile is **Giralda Plaza** (MAP: 11 P118 G2), a lively, car-free promenade lined with eateries and bars. During the evenings, string lights illuminate the street, creating a perfect ambience for a relaxed night out. If you visit during Giralda Live, held every first Friday of the month, the entire plaza transforms into an open-air dining room with live music. Pro tip: stop by **Café Demetrio** (MAP: 12 P118 G2; *cafedemetrio.com*), housed in a historic 1920s building, for a perfect *cortadito* or a quiet reading break. Free street parking is rare, but there are plenty of garages nearby. For a scenic detour, head east toward **Ponce Circle Park** (MAP: 13 P118 G3), where a grand statue of George Merrick watches over his masterpiece.

Play a Round at Granada Golf Course

SPORTS & RECREATION

MAP: 14 P118 D2

Golf courses don't get much more accessible – or historic – than **Granada Golf Course** (*golfcoralgables.com; 9 holes from $21*), Coral Gables' oldest public course. Established in 1923 this nine-hole, par-36 course is a scenic and budget-friendly way to experience the city's lush, Mediterranean-inspired landscapes. The course weaves through tree-lined fairways, past grand old homes and under the towering spire of the nearby Biltmore Hotel.

While it may not have the prestige of the adjacent Biltmore Golf Course, Granada offers a relaxed, welcoming atmosphere perfect for beginners and casual golfers. There's no tee time reservation required – just show up and play. If you'd rather spectate, grab a coffee at the clubhouse and watch locals perfect their swings. Keep an eye out for peacocks wandering the greens, a signature touch of Coral Gables' charm. For an early start, morning rounds often come with cooler temperatures and fewer crowds.

Snag a Selfie at the De Soto Fountain

HISTORY & ARCHITECTURE

MAP: 15 P118 **D3**

Few landmarks capture the elegance of Coral Gables quite like the **De Soto Fountain**. Built in 1925 as part of George Merrick's grand vision, this Mediterranean-style fountain serves as the entrance to the exclusive De Soto Boulevard and is one of the city's most photographed spots. Inspired by the grand fountains of Spanish and Italian plazas, it remains a symbol of the meticulous planning that shaped the 'City Beautiful.'

The fountain's coral rock base and pastel-hued stucco finish reflect the city's signature aesthetic, while its tranquil setting – surrounded by banyan trees and historic homes – makes it a perfect stop for a quiet moment or a photo op. It's an easy detour if you're exploring the nearby Venetian Pool, which is just down the road. While the fountain itself is purely decorative, the De Soto Plaza around it is a peaceful place to soak in Coral Gables' architectural beauty. For a full scenic route, drive or bike down De Soto Blvd, where some of the city's most spectacular mansions line the street.

Visit the Lowe Art Museum

ART & CULTURE

MAP: 16 P118 **D6**

Tucked inside the University of Miami's campus, the **Lowe Art Museum** *(lowe.miami.edu; adult/child $12.50/free)* is one of South Florida's oldest art institutions and home to an impressive 19,000-piece collection spanning everything from Renaissance paintings to contemporary glasswork. Established in 1950 it was the first art museum in Miami and remains a retreat for those looking to escape the city's more tourist-heavy attractions.

The museum's highlights include pre-Columbian artifacts, intricate Asian ceramics and a strong collection of European baroque and American modernist works. Art lovers will appreciate the Dale Chihuly glass sculptures, whose twisting, colorful forms add a contemporary edge to the classical surroundings. Unlike Miami's flashier art spaces, Lowe offers a quiet, intimate atmosphere – ideal for slow browsing. Free parking is available on campus, and admission is free on the first Tuesday of the month. If you visit on a weekday, the surrounding university grounds make for a peaceful stroll after your museum visit.

LISTINGS

Best Places for...

$ Budget $$ Midrange $$$ Top End

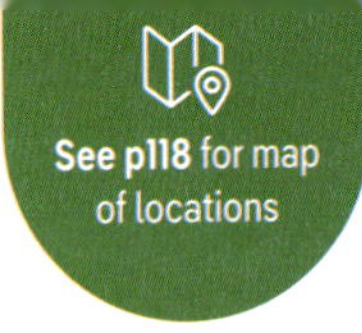

Eating

Bakeries

Madruga Bakery $

 17 B6

Come for craft breads and divine chocolate and hazelnut croissants. *madrugaorders.square.site, hours vary*

Bachour $

18 G1

Viennoiseries almost too beautiful to pick apart and eat delight the senses at this industrial-aesthetic bakery. *antoniobachour.com, 7am-7pm*

L'Artisane Bakery & Bistro $

19 G2

Come for French-style pastries, quiche and the sinfully good Biscoff cookie butter croissants. *lartisanebakery.com, hours vary*

Coral Bagels $

 20 H4

They are bagels, they are cheap and they are also very, very good at this family-owned shop. *coralbagels.com, 7am-3pm*

Worthy Splurges

Shingo $$$

21 H1

Omakase spot in Coral Gables with just 14 seats, where almost all the fish is fresh from Japan. *shingomiami.com, 6-11pm Tue-Sat*

Luca Osteria $$$

 22 G2

A *Chopped* winner helms this Italian restaurant known for pasta and negronis in a pedestrian zone of Coral Gables. *lucamiami.com, hours vary*

Romantic

Fontana $$

23 C4

Nestled within the historic Biltmore Hotel, an elegant courtyard dining experience around a charming fountain, with fine Italian cuisine. *biltmorehotel.com, hours vary*

NOMA Beach $$

24 H6

On the waterfront; a modern Italian seafood menu curated by Chef Donatella Arpaia. *noma-beach.com, hours vary*

Zucca $$

 25 G1

In the heart of Coral Gables, an authentic Italian dining experience complemented by an extensive wine list. *zuccamiami.com, hours vary*

Bulla Gastrobar $$

 26 G2

A vibrant atmosphere with a contemporary take on Spanish tapas. *bullagastrobar.com, hours vary*

Drinking

Divey & Casual

The Bar

27 G2

With a name like The Bar, you can count on this spot to be divey, laid-back and big on cold brews and burgers. Very affordable, too. *3pm-3am*

Seven Seas

 28 A2

Nautical-themed neighborhood dive in Coral Gables where you're sure to rub shoulders with many walks of life. *noon-3am*

Titanic Brewing Company

B6

Brewpub near the University of Miami that's bound to be going off any night of the week, with daily happy hour specials. *titanicbrewery.com, 11:30am-midnight Sun-Thu, to 1am Fri & Sat*

Loungey

Copper 29

30 G2

Retro Coral Gables gastropub on Miracle Mile with DJs, craft cocktails and even bottle service for those who wouldn't have it another way. *copper29bar.com, hours vary*

Fox's Lounge

A6

A South Miami staple since 1946, offering great food, stiff drinks and daily specials in a cozy, retro atmosphere. *foxslounge.com, 4pm-2am*

Don't Tell Papi

G2

Stylish mixology cocktail lounge and speakeasy with a New York vibe, accessible via an alley entrance marked by a barber sign. *hours vary*

Live Music

The Globe

F1

Live jazz on Saturdays, a lively bar and Euro cafe undertones make The Globe a perennial pick. *theglobecafe.com, hours vary*

The Biltmore Bar

C4

Sophisticated wood-paneled lounge featuring premium liquors, vintage wines and live music on weekends. *biltmorehotel.com, 4pm-midnight Tue-Thu, to 2am Fri & Sat*

Shopping

Shopping Centers

Miracle Mile

see 

G2

A vibrant stretch of boutiques, jewelers and upscale retailers, perfect for strolling, shopping and dining in one stretch. *hours vary*

Shops at Merrick Park

35 G6

Open-air luxury mall featuring high-end brands, designer boutiques and elegant dining. *shopsatmerrickpark.com, 11am-8pm Mon-Thu, to 9pm Fri & Sat, to 6pm Sun*

Giralda Plaza

see 11 G2

Pedestrian-friendly promenade lined with trendy shops, art galleries and lively restaurants, ideal for an afternoon of browsing. *hours vary*

Art

ArtLabbé Gallery

see 

G2

Contemporary gallery showcasing Latin American and European artists, specializing in abstract and modern works. *artlabbe.cl, hours vary*

Virginia Miller

36 G1

Colorful gallery with five decades-plus showcasing local art, often with an international or Latin flair. *virginiamiller.com, noon-6pm Tue-Fri*

Cernuda Arte

G4

Premier gallery specializing in Cuban art, from colonial-era pieces to contemporary works. *cernudaarte.com, 10:30am-6pm Mon-Sat*

H. Benitez Fine Art Gallery

G2

Intimate space highlighting bold, expressive paintings and sculptures by namesake artist Humberto Benitez. *humbertobenitez.com, hours vary*

★ WORTH A TRIP

Little Haiti, Upper East Side & Little River

These Miami neighborhoods are havens for rich Caribbean culture, retro-modern architecture and emerging creatives. Little Haiti pulses with the sounds of compas and street murals. The Upper East Side has striking Miami Modern (MiMo) architecture along Biscayne Boulevard. Meanwhile, Little River, once a quiet industrial zone, is now a creative hub with eclectic markets and boutiques.

PLANNING TIP
Each neighborhood has a distinct vibe that, combined, you can make a day of. Little Haiti and the Upper East Side shine in the daytime for architecture walks and Little River is primed for a leisurely afternoon of shopping and dining.

Scan this QR code for the latest Little Haiti Cultural Center events.

Little Haiti: Culture, Art & Vodou

Little Haiti is home to the largest Haitian community in North America, and its heart beats strongest at the **Little Haiti Cultural Center** *(miami.gov/LHCC)*. The center hosts rotating exhibitions, dance and drama performances and a Caribbean market where you can grab *epis,* the Haitian seasoning base. Next door, **Caribbean Marketplace** replicates Port-au-Prince's iconic Iron Market and is a great stop for handicrafts.

For a deeper dive into the neighborhood's Afro-Caribbean spiritual roots, visit one of the area's botanicas, which sell items tied to Vodou traditions. Don't believe the Hollywood stereotypes – Vodou here is a way of life, and many shops feature loa statues representing spirits that protect and guide their followers. Literature lovers should drop by **Libreri Mapou**, a cozy bookstore specializing in French, English and Haitian Creole works.

Upper East Side: MiMo & Modern Luxury

Spanning Biscayne Blvd from 50th to 77th Sts, the Upper East Side is an architectural treasure trove of Miami Modern (MiMo) design. Once a hot spot for mid-century travelers, the area's retro-glam

OLGA V KULAKOVA/SHUTTERSTOCK

hotels and diners have been restored, with spots like the **Vagabond Motel** (pictured) and **MiMo Biscayne Boulevard Historic District** offering a nostalgic nod to Miami's past. **Upper Buena Vista**, an outdoor shopping enclave, brings a touch of 'banyan-chic,' with massive trees shading locally owned boutiques selling unique home goods, jewelry and fashion. **Sweat Records**, a beloved indie record shop, has been a fixture for nearly two decades.

Little River: The Next Big Thing

Bordering Little Haiti, Little River is the city's rising creative playground. Formerly a warehouse district, it now features a mix of stylish markets and cutting-edge concept stores. Start at **The Citadel**, a food hall and market housing a rotating roster of top local chefs. Then, check out **Walter's Mercado**, a curated retail space where fashion meets global design, and **Mids Market**, a paradise for thrift lovers and DIY designers, complete with a 'rework station' where you can upcycle your finds.

QUICK BREAK
Imperial Moto is an unexpected specialty coffee shop, with its own roasted beans as well as classic motorcycles to gawk at throughout its hip space. Its pastries and cold brews will get your engine going.

★ WORTH A TRIP

Everglades

Across a massive South Florida mass stretches Everglades National Park *(nps.gov; individual/vehicle $20/35)*, a quiet wonderland of marshland, sawgrass and mangroves. You can hike, airboat, canoe, kayak or even travel by tram within it. There are four entrances in total to the park, the most popular, Shark Valley, being within a 45-minute drive of Downtown Miami.

PLANNING TIP
Rent a car for the day for ease of traveling to and within the Everglades. It gives you more freedom to explore the quirky roadside attractions, various trails and serene landscapes.

Scan this QR code for the latest park tours and closures.

A One-of-a-Kind Wilderness

There is no wilderness in the world quite like the Everglades. Called the 'River of Grass' by Native American inhabitants, it's not just a wetland, lake, river or grassland – it's all of these, twisted into a series of soft horizons, long vistas and sunsets stretching across your entire field of vision. The park's quiet majesty is evident in the sight of an anhinga opening glistening wings to the sun after a midmorning feed or in the slow, rhythmic flap of a great blue heron gliding over a mirror-like prairie. Out on Florida Bay, the marsh gives way to shallow seabeds where manatees bubble to the surface and aquatic birds nest by the thousands. The Everglades continues to face threats from encroaching development, invasive species and agriculture, but thanks to tireless conservation efforts, its importance is no longer in doubt. Beyond recreation, it's vital for regional water storage and flood control.

Geography & Entrances: Four Ways into the Wild

Everglades National Park covers 1.5 million acres, making it the third-largest national park in the

FRANCISCO BLANCO/SHUTTERSTOCK

continental US. There are four main entrances, each offering distinct experiences. The **Shark Valley Visitor Center**, west of Miami, serves as a gateway to Shark River Slough, home to the famous 15-mile paved Tram Road, ideal for biking and tram tours. The **Gulf Coast Visitor Center** in Everglades City is a hub for boating excursions into the Ten Thousand Islands, a labyrinth of mangrove islets and a wildlife refuge for thousands of birds. Just outside Homestead, the **Royal Palm Visitor Center** provides access to shorter hiking trails, including boardwalk paths through sawgrass marshes. The **Flamingo Visitor Center**, located 40 miles southwest of Royal Palm, is a launch point for paddling trails, manatee-spotting and backcountry camping. To make the most of an Everglades trip, visiting all four entrances is ideal.

QUICK BREAK
West of Homestead, the **Robert is Here Fruit Stand and Farm** is a statewide icon for uniquely fresh and exotic fruits, smoothies and milkshakes.

LORE AMID THE LUSHNESS
The Everglades' remoteness fuels eerie tales. Al Capone allegedly made moonshine in the Lost City. Hauntings persist near Eastern Airlines Flight 401's crash site.

Cycling & Tramming Through Shark Valley

The major destination for many visitors to the Everglades is **Shark Valley**, named not for its marine life but for its location at the headwaters of the little-known Shark River, which drains into the Gulf of Mexico. The big draw is the 15-mile paved loop trail that takes you deep into Shark River Slough. Along the way, you'll pass small creeks, tropical forests and borrow pits, human-made holes now home to basking gators, turtles and wading birds. The highlight of the trail is the 45ft **Shark Valley Observation Tower** (pictured), a brutalist concrete structure offering panoramic views of the River of Grass. The pancake-flat trail is ideal for cycling and bikes can be rented at the visitor center. Alternatively, a two-hour **tram**

tour, led by knowledgeable and oft-entertaining guides, provides an easy way to explore. If there's only time for one Everglades activity, this should be it. Booking a bike or tram tour in advance is recommended, especially during winter when the park is busiest.

The Miccosukee Tribe & Cultural Center

The Everglades has been inhabited for more than 15,000 years, long before European colonization. Today the **Miccosukee Indian Village** *(micco sukee.com; adult/child $15/10)*, located less than a half-mile from Shark Valley, offers insight into the history and legacy of the Miccosukee people. The village features a museum with beadwork, photographs and artifacts, as well as ethical

TAKMAT71/SHUTTERSTOCK

GETTING THERE
Getting to Shark Valley from Downtown Miami is easy – just a 40-minute drive west via US-41 (Tamiami Trail). There's no public transit, so drive or take a tour. For the Royal Palm entrance, head 55 minutes south via US-1 to FL-9336. The Everglades City and Flamingo entrances are 1½ hours away.

AFMARCOS/SHUTTERSTOCK

ALLIGATORS & CROCS

The Everglades is the only place where American alligators and crocodiles coexist. Alligators are darker with broad snouts, living in freshwater, while crocodiles are lighter with narrow snouts, thriving in both fresh and saltwater.

alligator demonstrations that emphasize the cultural importance of these creatures. There are also storytelling sessions, native crafts and traditional foods available. The Miccosukee also operate the **Miccosukee Casino & Resort**, located about 20 miles east along the Tamiami Trail, offering another aspect of the culture.

Airboat Rides: The Everglades' Signature Ride

If the Everglades had an official vehicle, it would be the airboat. Along the Tamiami Trail, airboat tour signs line the roadside, advertising rides on these flat-bottomed boats powered by massive propeller fans. Airboats skim effortlessly over the grass- and lily-filled waters, providing an accessible way to experience the Everglades' wildlife. The soundtrack of the ride is the hum of the propeller, the occasional splash of water and the calls of unseen birds. Only three companies operate within the national park itself: **Gator Park** *(gatorpark.com)*, **Everglades Safari Park** *(evergladessafaripark.com)*, and **Coopertown Airboats** *(coopertownairboats.com)*. Outside the park, numerous other operators run airboat tours, with most boats holding a dozen or so passengers under a shaded canopy. Some companies offer private, small-group tours for a more intimate experience. For families with children, it's wise to sit toward the middle of the boat to prevent little hands from reaching for the wildlife.

Boating Through the 10,000 Islands

The **Ten Thousand Islands** is one of the most breathtaking wilderness areas in Florida, where a maze of mangrove islets stretches as far as the eye can see. The best way to explore is by boat. The Gulf Coast Visitor Center in Everglades City is the main launch point for water excursions. While the center has suffered recent hurricane damage, tours still run through **Everglades Florida Adventures** *(evergladesfloridaadventures.com)*, which offers 90-minute catamaran trips through Chokoloskee Bay and Indian Key Pass. For a more hands-on adventure, kayak and canoe rentals are available for anything from a few hours to multiday expeditions. Guided paddle tours, offered by **Everglades Adventures Kayak & Eco Tours** *(evergladesadventures.com)*, range from two- to three-hour excursions to overnight camping trips on remote islands. Wildlife sightings in the Ten Thousand Islands are unmatched, with bottlenose dolphins gliding through the waters, ospreys and bald eagles soaring overhead, loggerhead turtles nesting on sandy islands, and great blue herons, alligators and even the rare American crocodile lurking in the shallows.

GUARDIAN OF THE GLADES

Marjory Stoneman Douglas championed Everglades conservation long before it was popular. Her 1947 book *The Everglades: River of Grass* reframed the wetlands as a national treasure. In 1969 she founded Friends of the Everglades, a nonprofit still fighting for its preservation.

WHO CREATED THE AIRBOAT?

Alexander Graham Bell designed the first airboat, *Ugly Duckling*, in 1905. Though slow, it allowed safer water travel. By the 1930s Floridians refined the design, making it the Everglades' go-to transport.

★ WORTH A TRIP

Key Biscayne

Floating like a glittering residential jewel in the bay it is named for, Key Biscayne and neighboring Virginia Key are a quick and easy getaway from Downtown Miami. Once you pass some scenic causeways, you'll feel like you've left Miami for a floating suburb with magnificent beaches, lush nature trails in state parks and aquatic adventures aplenty.

PLANNING TIP
The best way to explore is by car or bike as public transit is limited. Arrive early to snag parking, especially on weekends. Bring bug spray for nature trails.

A Quiet Escape with a Wild Side

Among the naturescapes here, **Virginia Key Beach North Point Park** is a peaceful green space with small, uncrowded beaches and short nature trails. The main draw is renting kayaks or paddleboards from the **Virginia Key Outdoor Center**. Paddle through mangrove tunnels or into the bay, where dolphins and manatees often appear. The park also features some of the region's best off-road biking trails, winding through coastal hammocks and sandy stretches for a thrilling ride.

Though much of Virginia Key remains undeveloped, it is home to the graffiti-covered Miami Marine Stadium, a relic of a bygone era that once hosted powerboat races and concerts, and remains a favorite among photographers and urban explorers.

The Crown Jewel of Key Biscayne

Crandon Park is a 1200-acre expanse of coastal hammock, mangrove swamps and a pristine 2-mile-long beach. Unlike the crowded shores of South Beach, Crandon's sands are quiet, offering a more relaxed, natural experience. The shallow, calm water makes it perfect for families and swimmers looking for a peaceful retreat. Once home to Miami's only zoo, remnants of its past remain in the abandoned wildlife enclosures hidden in the

Scan this QR code for area maps and visitor information.

OCUDRONE/SHUTTERSTOCK

trees. Beyond the beach, Crandon's nature trails provide a shaded escape into South Florida's ecosystem, with boardwalks weaving through dense mangrove forests. For a different perspective on this stretch of the bay, rent a kayak or paddleboard and explore the waters from offshore.

A Window into South Florida's Wild Side

Tucked within Crandon Park, the **Marjory Stoneman Douglas Biscayne Nature Center** is a great stop for families and nature lovers alike. The center features hands-on exhibits, small aquariums filled with local marine life and guided nature walks through coastal hammocks and seagrass beds. Educational programs highlight Biscayne Bay's delicate ecosystem. Just beyond the center, a quiet beach offers another chance to wade into clear, shallow waters where fish dart past your feet, making this a place to both learn and connect with the natural beauty of Key Biscayne.

QUICK BREAK
Refuel at **La Boulangerie Boul'Mich**, a cozy French-Latin cafe known for its flaky croissants and rich café con leche – a nice post-Key Biscayne recharge before heading back to the mainland.

#unlockmiami
citibike

Miami Toolkit

LAZYLLAMA/SHUTTERSTOCK

Family Travel

Miami has plenty of attractions for young travelers, including beautiful beaches, grassy parks, nature trails, megamalls and zoos. Animal-centric experiences are easy to find, and there's no shortage of great snacks, from Italian-style gelato to Venezuelan *arepas*. The city also offers numerous family-friendly hotels and restaurants.

Beaching on a Budget

Family travel in Miami can be affordable with free beaches, parks and scenic promenades. Opt for lodging with a kitchen to save on meals. Many attractions, including major museums, offer free-entry days or group discounts, making it easy to enjoy the city without breaking the budget.

KIDS' FACILITIES

Many hotels offer cribs, highchairs, babysitting and even kids' clubs, while restaurants typically accommodate kids. Attractions have stroller-friendly paths, and public beaches feature playgrounds, shaded areas and family restrooms, making outings with little ones more convenient and enjoyable.

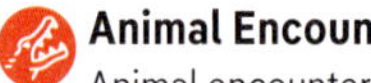

Animal Encounters

Animal encounters in Miami and broader South Florida are common, be it snorkeling excursions or seeing alligators sunbathing by a random lake. In terms of organized programs that are supervised by trained staff, children should obey all guidelines. Out in the wild, all wildlife should be left alone, and children should steer clear.

Year-Round Fun

Greater Miami Convention & Visitors Bureau *(miamiandbeaches.com)* keeps an updated, year-round guide on the latest family-friendly events and festivals.

Children's Discounts

Kids often get free or discounted public transport fares, group rates at attractions, and savings with passes like Go City Miami.

Airboat Rides With Kids

Airboat rides in the Everglades are an exciting family adventure. Kids should stay seated and follow guides' instructions. Bring child-sized ear protection, sunscreen, hats and bug spray. Opt for family-friendly tours with experienced guides for a safe, fun experience.

Accommodations

A Miami stay is as swanky as you want it to be, spanning cozy single-level home rentals, restored art deco hotels and lux resorts with all the amenities.

Where to Stay if You Love...

Sun, Sand & Neon

Miami Beach (p35) Iconic for its art deco hotels, lively Ocean Dr and beach access; the go-to area for sun-seekers and party lovers. Options span budget hostels to luxury beachfront resorts.

Skyscrapers & a Central Location

Downtown Miami (p53) Packed with high-rise hotels, museums and top restaurants. Easy access to the Kaseya Center, Bayfront Park and public transit hubs. Tall modern hotels, catering to business and leisure travelers alike.

Street Art & Indie Vibes

Wynwood (p73) The edgy epicenter of Miami's art scene, Wynwood is filled with colorful murals, craft breweries and hip nightlife. A small selection of smaller hotels and loft-style stays cater to those who want creative surrounds.

Cuban Culture & Dancing

Little Havana (p93) Latin music, *ventanitas* for snagging a *cafecito* and historic landmarks make it a melting pot like few others. Small hotels and hotels provide a no-frills stay.

A Quieter yet Lux Retreat

Coral Gables (p117) Coral Gables is elegant and comparatively quiet. Home to lush gardens and upscale-vibed streets. Expect charming boutique hotels with a more relaxed ambience.

We Love to Stay in...

Miami Beach (p35) When people think of Miami, it's the white sands, people-watching, neon lights and thumping nights. So, why not just stay in the heart of it? Fun fact: Miami Beach is its own city, separate from Miami, very much with its own beach-y aroma and infrastructure. While not nearly as large as Miami proper, it's the perfectly vibrant home base.

HOW MUCH FOR A NIGHT IN

Hostel dorm bed from **$30**

Boutique midrange hotel from **$150**

Luxury beachfront resort from **$300**

Food, Drink & Nightlife

Allergies & Intolerances

Miami's diverse food scene means plenty of options, but those with allergies should always double-check. Many menus openly list allergens, especially in high-end and health-conscious restaurants. Additionally, most restaurants will ask if diners have any allergies pre-meal. If in doubt, inform your server.

Cafecito Culture

The Cuban *cafecito*, a small but powerful shot of espresso sweetened with sugar, is served from walk-up windows called *ventanitas*, found all over the city. Locals take their coffee seriously, whether it's a quick *colada* (shared shot of *cafecito*) or a smooth *cortadito* (espresso with a dash of milk).

WATER CHOICES

At most Miami restaurants, you'll have the option between still, sparkling and tap water. Still and sparkling water almost always come with a charge.

DRESS THE PART

While Miami is a generally casual-meets-stylish destination, some restaurants do have strict dress codes. Common no-nos in higher-end establishments include no wearing of baseball caps, swim trunks and/or flip-flops. When in doubt, ask a restaurant about its attire restrictions while booking or check its website.

Reservations

Booking ahead is recommended, especially for dinner at popular spots in Miami Beach, Wynwood and Brickell. Many upscale restaurants require a credit card to secure a reservation. Walk-ins are more common at casual Cuban cafes and taco joints but wait times can be long at peak hours.

HOW TO... Pay the Bill

Your bill will usually be brought to your table either at the end of your meal or by requesting it. Payment is expected shortly thereafter, particularly in busier restaurants.

Splitting the bill Some restaurants allow it, but it's best to let your server know as soon as you are seated. Many upscale venues may only allow one credit card per table.

Tipping Service isn't always included. A tip of 15% to 20% or higher is standard in Miami restaurants. Some places, especially in Miami Beach, may automatically add gratuity, so check your bill before tipping extra.

PRICE RANGES

The following price ranges reflect the average cost of a main course in Miami.
$ less than $15
$$ $15–35
$$$ more than $35

OPENING HOURS

Cafes 7am–6pm
Restaurants 11am–10pm, though some stay open later
Fast Food 11am to midnight or later

Going Out

The Nightlife Scene Legendary, with options from high-energy nightclubs to hidden cocktail lounges. Miami Beach is famous for megaclubs, Wynwood has intimate music venues like Gramps and Downtown is home to 24/7 megaclub E11EVEN Miami.

When to Go Clubs don't start filling up until after midnight, with peak hours between 1am and 3am.

At the Door Dress codes are strict in high-end clubs – expect to wear heels or collared shirts. Some venues require table reservations for large groups, and getting past the doorman can be tough if you are not on your A game.

What to Drink Miami's most popular drinks include mojitos, piña coladas, espresso martinis and the classic Cuba libre. Cocktail bars serve craft rum-based drinks, while beachside spots favor frozen daiquiris and margaritas. Miami has a stellar craft beer scene, too, with Wynwood Brewing, Cervecería La Tropical and J. Wakefield being local favorites.

HOW MUCH FOR A

Dinner for two at a Michelin-star restaurant
$700–800

Slice of key lime pie
$7–10

Cafecito
$1–3

Specialty coffee
$6–8

Bottle of beer
$7–9

Glass of wine
$10–12

Cuban sandwich
$10–12

Pound of stone crabs
$70–90

PIXEL-SHOT/SHUTTERSTOCK

LGBTIQ+ Travelers

Despite state politics, Miami remains a top LGBTIQ+ destination, with inclusive communities and a vibrant, welcoming scene.

Gayborhoods

Miami Beach is the city's ultimate LGBTIQ+ hot spot, especially around 12th St & Ocean Dr, where sporadic rainbow flags mark the lively beach scene. The area is packed with high-energy clubs, drag brunches and oceanfront cocktail bars, making it the heart of Miami's gay nightlife.

Wynwood attracts a progressive, creative crowd, blending art, music and inclusive spaces. LGBTIQ+-friendly bars, underground speakeasies and energetic drag shows – particularly at **R House** (p83), known for its lively drag brunch – help define the neighborhood's scene.

Downtown and Brickell offer a more polished, upscale vibe, featuring stylish rooftop lounges, craft cocktails and all-night parties. **Club Space** and **Blackbird Ordinary** (p71) are two favorites known for their diverse, welcoming crowds and vibrant nightlife.

OUR PICKS

By Day of the Week

TUESDAY Trivia Night at Nathan's Bar A campy, drag-hosted trivia night with cocktails and laughs.

WEDNESDAY Drag Bingo at Hotel Gaythering Hilarious performances, cheeky prizes and a lively crowd.

THURSDAY Double Stubble at Gramps (p84) Wynwood's iconic queer night with DJs and live music.

FRIDAY Midnight Latin Nights at Azucar Drag, reggaeton and nonstop dancing.

PRIDE

Every April Miami Beach Pride transforms Ocean Dr into a rainbow-filled celebration with parades, beach parties and drag. The events attract 200,000 attendees for a high-energy week.

A WINTER PARTY

A pre-Pride party, Winter Party, held in February/March, attracts thousands for a week of beach parties, dance events and LGBTIQ+ celebrations.

Resources

LGBT Visitor Center A go-to for Miami's LGBTIQ+ scene. *gogaymiami.com* • **Greater Miami Convention & Visitors Bureau LGBTIQ+ Guide** A comprehensive guide to Miami's gay-friendly attractions. *miamiandbeaches.com* • **hotspotsmagazine.com** South Florida staple LGBTIQ+ publication with nightlife, culture and community news.

Health & Safe Travel

Miami is a big city with typical big-city crime issues. Stay vigilant and street-smart to ensure your 'fun in the sun' isn't ruined.

INSURANCE

Florida doesn't require travel insurance, but with high US healthcare costs, coverage is a smart choice. Opt for a plan that includes lost luggage, trip cancellations and adventure activities like diving and boating for added protection.

Hurricanes

South Florida has been prone to hurricanes in recent years, especially during hurricane season, which spans from June to November, often peaking in August and September. These storms bring heavy rain, strong winds and storm surges that can cause significant damage and pose serious risks to safety. Residents and visitors alike must stay informed and follow all official directives during storm emergencies to protect themselves and others.

Tap Water

Miami's tap water is safe to drink but may have a mineral taste, leading some visitors to prefer bottled water.

Jellyfish & Sea Urchins

These creatures can wash near shore, especially after storms Stings are painful but rarely dangerous. Remove tentacles or spines with tweezers, soak in hot water and use vinegar for jellyfish stings. Seek medical attention for severe pain, allergic reactions or embedded spines.

CANNABIS

Recreational cannabis is illegal in Florida. Only medical marijuana patients can purchase legally. Possession of up to 20g is a misdemeanor, with potential fines or jail time.

QUICK INFO

Drinks

Be vigilant of drink spiking in bars and clubs.

Security

Always lock bicycles, in both low- and high-traffic areas.

Pedestrians

Have the right of way, but stay aware for aggressive drivers, even within cross-walks.

FROM LEFT: NEW AFRICA/SHUTTERSTOCK, TAMARA KULIKOVA/SHUTTERSTOCK

Responsible Travel

Follow these tips to leave a lighter footprint, support local businesses and have a positive impact on communities.

Volunteer

If you're looking to give back while visiting Miami, there are plenty of opportunities to volunteer with organizations dedicated to preserving the area's unique ecosystems.

Consider **Miami Waterkeeper** (*miamiwaterkeeper.org*), which champions clean water and a healthy marine ecosystem in Miami and beyond. Volunteers help with beach cleanups, mangrove plantings and advocacy initiatives designed to keep local waterways pollution-free.

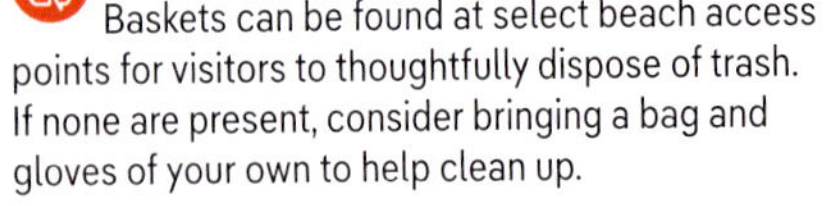

Clean Beaches

Baskets can be found at select beach access points for visitors to thoughtfully dispose of trash. If none are present, consider bringing a bag and gloves of your own to help clean up.

OUR PICK

Our Pick: Eco-Friendly Stays

Choose accommodations certified for sustainability, like **1 Hotel South Beach**, which is as eco-driven as it is eco-chic.

Vroom Vroom

Use eco-friendly transportation whenever possible. Consider biking (rentals are abundant throughout the city) or walking whenever traveling short distances. Most areas in the city are very bike friendly, though stay vigilant.

Canoes and kayaks are also widely available for rent at state parks and select hotels, making for a unique and relaxed way of getting around.

Airboats are widespread and an integral part of life in South Florida, as well as an important way for people of all abilities to experience these unique wetlands. However, there are concerns about their use: they are noisy and create a significant disturbance to local wildlife. We recommend researching airboat tours before booking and considering alternatives like paddle boat tours or on-land bicycle or walking tours.

SNORKEL & DIVE RESPONSIBLY

Book a Blue Star-recognized dive or snorkel operator, meaning the company promotes and adheres to sustainable practices designed to mitigate harm to coral reefs.

Respect the Sea Turtles

Sea turtles are a fascinating sight in Miami, especially during nesting season, from May to October. However, it's essential to respect their space, as disturbing them is not only harmful but also illegal. Avoid getting too close, shining lights or using flash photography, as these can disorient mother turtles and hatchlings trying to reach the ocean. Many coastal hotels and businesses use special orange-hued lighting to prevent disrupting their natural environment. If you encounter a nesting turtle or hatchlings, observe from a distance and allow nature to take its course.

LOCAL INDIGENOUS COMMUNITIES

Venture to the **Miccosukee Indian Village** (p137) for authentic cultural experiences that honor Native American history. Any funds or proceeds benefit the tribe directly.

Resources

Wearefcc.org The Florida Conservation Coalition.

Eco-usa.net/orgs/fl.shtml Alphabetical list of Florida's environmental organizations.

Everglades Coalition Non-profit focused on protecting and restoring the Everglades.

Climate Change & Travel

It's impossible to ignore the impact we have when traveling; Lonely Planet urges all travelers to engage with their travel carbon footprint, which will mainly come from air travel. While there often isn't an alternative, travelers can look to minimize the number of flights they take, opt for newer aircraft and use cleaner ground transport, such as trains. One proposed solution – purchasing carbon offsets – unfortunately does not cancel out the impact of individual flights. While most destinations will depend on air travel for the foreseeable future, for now, pursuing ground-based travel where possible is the best course of action.

The **UN Carbon Offset Calculator** shows how flying impacts a household's emissions.

The **ICAO's carbon emissions calculator** allows visitors to analyze the CO2 generated by point-to-point journeys.

Accessible Travel

ADA-Friendly Beaches

Many of the most popular beaches are wheelchair-accessible, featuring ramp access to boardwalks. Several offer complimentary beach wheelchairs and Mobi-Mats: interlocking pads that create a solid path over the sand. On Miami Beach, beaches like **Crandon Park** (p140) provide accessible paths and manual beach wheelchairs.

Mobile on the High Seas

Mobility challenges needn't restrict fun on the water. Accessible catamarans and adaptive sailing and boating experiences are widely available throughout the Sunshine State, with providers like **Shake-A-Leg Miami** *(shakealegmiami.org)* making excursions easy and enjoyable.

Vizcaya Museum & Gardens (p105) has a blend of history and nature, and ensures accessibility for all visitors. The estate has wheelchair-accessible paths through its vivid gardens, allowing guests to explore the serene landscapes with ease. Inside the historic mansion an elevator grants access to key areas, and Braille guides help visually impaired visitors navigate the space. Assistive Listening Devices (ALDs) are available for tours and service animals are welcomed.

VISUALLY IMPAIRED VISITORS

Braille guides and signs are increasingly common at tourist attractions. State law mandates that all public facilities allow trained service dogs, a requirement widely embraced by Florida's many pet-friendly business owners.

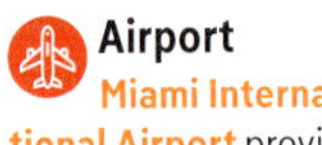

Airport

Miami International Airport provides barrier-free paths and accessible services throughout its terminals, including guided mobility assistance at designated locations. If a wheelchair is required upon arrival, request it in advance.

ASSISTIVE LISTENING DEVICES

Many attractions offer sign-language services with advance booking. **Pérez Art Museum Miami** (p56) provides Assistive Listening Devices (ALDs), and printed guides are often available for museum and gallery tours.

Resources

- **Visit Florida** *(visitflorida.com/things-to-do/accessible-travel)* provides an extensive list of accessible Miami attractions along with resources for wheelchair and scooter rentals, childcare services and oxygen supplies.

Nuts & Bolts

Opening Hours

Banks 9am–5pm, Monday–Friday. Some branches open Saturday mornings.

Museums Typically 10am–5pm; some have extended evening hours on specific days. Many are closed on Mondays.

Restaurants Lunch noon–3pm, dinner 5–10pm. Casual spots and bars may stay open much later.

Shops 10am–8pm, Monday–Saturday. Some operate on Sundays.

Bars/Clubs Many are open until 2am, some until 5am or later.

QUICK INFO

Time Zone Eastern Standard Time

City Calling Code 305 and 786

Emergency Number 911

Population 2.7 million

ELECTRICITY

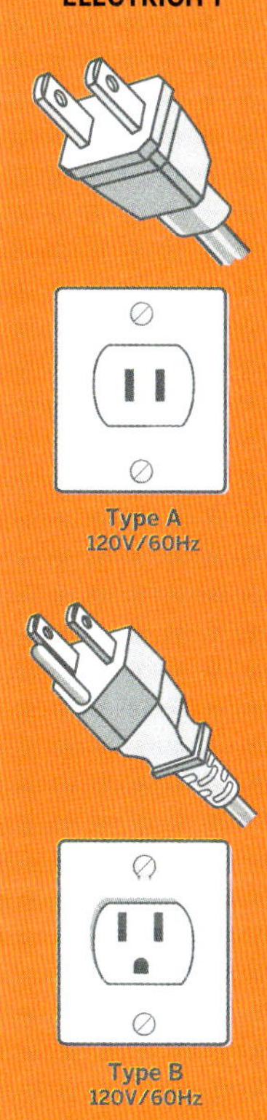

Public Holidays

Eight public holidays are recognized throughout the year in Florida. On these dates, government offices and most businesses (except essential services) are closed.

New Year's Day January 1

Martin Luther King Jr Day Third Monday of January

Memorial Day Final Monday of May

Independence Day July 4

Labor Day First Monday of September

Veterans Day November 11

Thanksgiving Fourth Thursday of November

Christmas December 25 (If Christmas falls on a Sunday, the following Monday is also a recognized holiday.)

Smoking & Vaping

Smoking is prohibited in most indoor businesses, including restaurants and bars. Many Miami beaches and parks also ban smoking to reduce litter. Vaping often falls under the same restrictions, so check local ordinances or signage before using e-cigarettes.

Index

See also separate subindexes for:
Eating p156
Drinking p157
Shopping p157

Sights p000 Map pages p000

Eating

Drinking

Shopping

Send Us Your Feedback

We love to hear from travellers – your comments help make our books better. We read every word, and we guarantee that your feedback goes straight to the authors. Visit lonelyplanet.com/contact to submit your updates and suggestions.

Note: We may edit, reproduce and incorporate your comments in Lonely Planet products such as guidebooks, websites and digital products, so let us know if you are happy to have your name acknowledged. For a copy of our privacy policy visit lonelyplanet.com/legal.

Acknowledgements

Cover photograph: Colony Hote (p41). Susanne Kremer/4Corner Images

Back photograph: Lifeguard tower, Wirestock Creators/ Shutterstock

THIS BOOK

Destination Editor
Caroline Trefler

Cartographer
Rachel Imeson

Production Editors
Katie Connolly, Kate James

Book Designer
Nicolas D'Hoedt

Coordinating Editor
Imogen Bannister

Assisting Editors
Charlotte Orr, Kathryn Rowan

Cover Researcher
Kat Marsh

Thanks to
Terry Ward for Miami source material

Published by Lonely Planet Global Limited
CRN 554153
3rd edition – September 2025
ISBN 978 1 83869 410 4

10 9 8 7 6 5 4 3 2 1
Printed in Malaysia